Murder in the Midlands

by Barrie Roberts

QuercuS

****

QuercuS
John Roberts
67, Cliffe Way, Warwick
CV34 5JG 01926 776363

****

Murder in the Midlands

by Barrie Roberts

ISBN 1 898136 19 X

First Published 2000

Preface

QuercuS specialises in publishing books about the western Midlands, or the area between the rivers Trent, Severn and Avon that geographers call the "Midland Triangle". Titles include *Midland Woods & Forests, Midland Rivers, Midland Ghosts & Hauntings, Midland Castles, Historic Houses & Gardens, Heart in my Boots, Coaching Days in the Midlands, Midland Murders & Mysteries, Midland Spirits & Spectres* and albums of pen and ink sketches of buildings in Hales Owen, Bromsgrove and Birmingham. Later came the autobiographies, *Us Kids* and *The Treacle Stick*.

Barrie Roberts was coauthor of both the ghost books, and realising how much he knew about the bizarre, the gruesome and the absurd, I asked him to write *Midland Murders* etc. It was so popular that I reprinted within twelve months and asked him to write this book.

The Author

BARRIE ROBERTS was born in Hampshire in 1939, but has lived in the Midlands for over thirty years. For most of that time he worked in criminal law for two firms of solicitors, working on a number of murder cases, major frauds and the appeals of the Birmingham Six.

He is now a writer and lecturer and his books include: *Sherlock Holmes and the Railway Maniac* (1994), *Sherlock Holmes and the Devil's Grail* (1996), *Sherlock Holmes and the Man from Hell* (1997), *Sherlock Holmes and the Royal Flush* (1998) and *Sherlock Holmes and the Harvest of Death (1999)*. He has added two modern mystery novels: *The Victory Snapshot (1998)* and *Robbery With Malice (1999)*. He was the coauthor with Anne Bradford of *Midland Ghosts and Hauntings* (Quercus, 1994) and *Midland Spirits and Spectres* (Quercus, 1997), then by himself wrote *Midland Murders & Mysteries,*

Barrie lectures for the City of Birmingham, teaching a long running course at Great Barr on Ghosts and Unsolved Mysteries. Apart from his professional involvement with the law, Barrie is a lifelong collector of accounts of crime cases and these cases come largely from his huge private library.

Sources & Acknowledgements

There is a large accumulation of books and cuttings about past crimes in my own library. However, for those of you who can't spare fifty years to make such a collection, let me name some of the other sources used in this book. No writer on murder can ignore the work of those who have gone before, and I have to acknowledge the help received from Michael Posner's *Midland Murders* (Star, 1973), Betty Smith's *Warwickshire Murders* (Countryside Books, 1991) W.M.Jamieson's *Murders, Myths and Monuments of North Staffordshire* (Westmid Supplies, 1979) and Brian Lane's *The Murder Club Guide to the Midlands* (Harrap, 1988). In all of them you will find cases which I have not included.

It is impossible to research the past of the West Midlands without looking at twenty five years of issues of the *Black Country Bugle*. This fascinating local weekly magazine roots indefatigably into stories of old crimes in its area, and often inspires readers to supply personal recollections and old documents.

There are too many Public Libraries in the region to mention, but I refer you to them, particularly Birmingham Reference Library, the Salt Library at Stafford and to the West Midlands Police Museum in Birmingham. I have also used anthologies like Patrick Wilson's *Murderess* (Michael Joseph, 1971), the *Notable British Trials* series and the *Penguin Famous Trials*. Then there are biographies such as Allen Andrews' biography of Mervyn Pugh, *The Prosecutor,* (Harrap, 1968) and Browne and Tullett's *Bernard Spilsbury: His Life and Cases* (Harrap, 1951).

Finally, the cover picture shows Lord Ferrers shooting his steward in 1760. A contemporary pen and ink sketch was in such poor condition as not to be worth printing, so what you see is a new version by artist Andy Tew of Warwick. We can tell you that his work shows considerably greater artistic skill than the original. You will find more of Andy sketches through the book and he deserves our thanks.

Barrie Roberts
2000

Contents

Introduction   1

"With intent to ravish" (Handsworth, Birmingham 1890)   3
"You have murdered me!" (Ranton, Staffs 1833)   8
"The brightest child of God." (Leicester 1832)   11
"They have got me!" (Coulonne, Belgium 1940)   17
"It was her fault." (Oldbury, Worcs 1913)   23

"A glass or two of brandy." (Oddingley, Worcs 1806)   28
"Time will reveal the dreadful secret." (Hayton, Notts 1937)   33
"With dog and gun and snare." (Ryton on Dunsmore, Warks 1858)   40
"A cure for the rankish itch." (Burntwood, Staffs 1843)   64
"Oh God! Is it my wife?" (Walsall & Birmingham 1964-69)   66

"Your time is come - you must die!" (Staunton Harold, Leics 1760)   82
"I should like to have my revenge." (Orgreave, Staffs 1895)   89
"A most terrible lesson." (Wolverhampton, Staffs 1908)   97
"Do you think I shall be hung? (Wychnor Bridges, Staffs 1816)   100
"Respectable and indulgent parents." (Swindon, Worcs 1808)   106

"He could thread a needle." (West Bromwich, Staffs 1933)   111
"Trifle not with young mens' feelings." (Aston, Birmingham 1877)   114

NB. The places are named with the counties they were in at the time to explain, for example, why a Dudley crime was tried in the Assize Court at Worcester, the County town.

Introduction

More than half a century ago George Orwell turned his mind to the subject of the English murder. He thought he had noticed a change in the patterns of the crime evidenced by the so called 'Cleft Chin Murder', in which an American deserter and a teenage English girl killed for a few pounds to spend on drinks and dance halls.

Orwell lamented the passing of 'real' English murders, the ones you could settle down to read in the *News of the World* after a solid Sunday lunch. His formula for a classic murder which was essentially that it should arise out of a guilty love affair, with the guilty party a pillar of the local chapel or a stalwart of the constituency Conservative party. Orwell wanted carefully planned, long nurtured crimes that only led to the gallows through that one fatal slip in preparation or commission. He deprecated the lack of deep motive and the careless execution in post war murders.

Anyone who reads newspapers knows that Orwell was wrong, there have always been murders with no significant motive. What may have been the Midlands' first serial killer struck centuries ago in a Coventry almshouse, killing eight of his fellow inmates by poisoning their porridge (a cereal killer?). Questioned about the deaths, he managed to divert suspicion, but then killed himself, leaving a note explaining that he had resented being the youngest member of the institution.

Feckless murder has always been with us and so has simple murder. The most common English murder arises when a relationship is subject to some real or imagined strain, one partner takes a rolling pin or a carving knife to the other and is quickly caught. Interesting cases are those where the relationships involved are unusual or complex, where the method of murder is uncommon or where there is a long hunt for the killer. Most English cases do not meet that specification, any more than they meet Orwell's, but there have always been a few that stand out from the general dullness.

This collection, then, is the result of sorting through centuries of crimes in the Midlands looking for the unusual. Here is the last peer to stand trial for murder before the House of Lords, here is a man who was, to all intents and purposes, tried in two different courts for the same murder, here is a man tried in Birmingham for a murder which (if there was a murder) was committed in France, here is a girl killed by an invisible man. As with my previous collection, *Midland Murders and Mysteries*, I have tried to give you variety and interest by recounting cases spread across two centuries.

Once again I should point out that I have included no case less that twenty five years old, partly because people remember them and partly because I have no wish to re-awaken recent pain in relatives and friends.

I must thank readers of the earlier book who have pointed me in the direction of particular cases. Especial thanks to Gary Moore of Nuneaton who made available his large file on the unsolved murder of his great grandfather, Joseph Owen. I am sorry that for reasons of space I had to shorten his detailed narrative, and ask his pardon. Many thanks also to Audrey Bayley, a long time student in my Birmingham evening class on Ghosts and Unsolved Mysteries. She gave me material on a murder in which one of her ancestors was neither killer nor victim, but the third party in a triangle. Thanks finally to my brother, the military historian Philip Roberts, for his help with the case of Corporal Mavity who either did or did not kill his commanding officer.

2

'With intent to ravish'
(Handsworth, Birmingham 1890)

Most English murders are quickly solved. They are not
the complex cases that we read about in thrillers or watch
on television. There are few of television's demonically
clever killers luring victims into extraordinary situations
and killing them by exotic means from some obscure
motive.

Most people are killed by a spouse or lover, friend or
acquaintance, which narrows the list of suspects. Most
of the motives are the simple ones of anger, lust, greed or
revenge. The weapon is usually a blunt instrument, a kitchen
knife or whatever is to hand when some old grievance finally
explodes. Scientific evidence is usually plentiful and when
confronted the murderer often confesses. What more could
a detective want, apart from actually being present when
the crime was committed?

When Matilda Crawford was murdered there was a detective,
only a couple of feet away, but there was never any hunt for
her killer and we do not know how she was killed, or even
whether she was actually murdered.

Walk down Soho Road, Handsworth in north Birmingham,
past its rows of Muslim, Sikh and West Indian shops, as rich
and exciting a mixture as you will find in England. Then look
at the few huge, decorative Victorian pubs and above the shop
fronts, and you will see the faded remains of expensive late
Victorian and Edwardian architecture, echoing a time when
Handsworth was a wealthy executive commuter suburb of
Birmingham.

Originally Handsworth was a tiny village in rural Staffordshire
whose only importance was that travellers to and from Ireland
could catch a coach there on the Holyhead Road. This changed
dramatically when the Great Western Railway built a line from
Wolverhampton to Birmingham with a station at Soho. Suddenly
wealthy manufacturers and their senior managers could live in
leafy Handsworth and take a train into Birmingham. Handsworth
blossomed and expanded to become part of the city.

At the height of this period, on Thursday 4th December 1890, Matilda Crawford set out from Wolverhampton on a train to Snow Hill, Birmingham. It was not scheduled to stop at Soho. Her carriage was not a modern open plan one with a central aisle, but an old fashioned carriage of separate compartments with a seat along each side and a door at each end. There was no corridor and the compartment doors opened directly to the outside.

Some of us still remember such carriages. A friend of mine was in a large party of evacuee children shipped in a train from London to Somerset in September 1939. With no corridor and no access to toilets, the trainful of frightened, excited children was awash by the time it reached Wantage, Berkshire. Here the train made an enforced emergency stop and here my friend spent the rest of the war.

Miss Crawford's problem was more serious. As her train rattled through Soho Station on its way to Snow Hill the lady fell out of a window, suffering serious injuries. She lived long enough to tell the Police that she had been assaulted by a fellow traveller. Once the train was moving a young man who shared her compartment had started to make unwelcome advances. He would not be put off and when she reached for the communication cord (introduced by Parliament after Franz Muller murdered Mr Briggs in a railway compartment in 1864), he had pushed her out of the window.

4

Matilda did not survive her injuries long and you might think that Victorian popular opinion would have been outraged, that the Police would have spared no effort until the pervert who had killed an innocent traveller was caught. This did not happen.

At the Inquest much of the evidence was beyond dispute. Matilda had boarded the Birmingham train at Wolverhampton and fallen from it at Soho. What threw the case into confusion and left it there was the evidence of a detective who had travelled on the same train.

He had been the first person to board the train at Wolverhampton, getting into the compartment next to Matilda's and sitting so that he was looking towards that compartment. He would have seen her fellow passenger and should have been able to provide a description, but he couldn't. He could only say that he saw Miss Crawford board the train and get into the compartment next to his, but no one else got into that compartment before the train left Wolverhampton. There had been no stop on the journey.

The Coroner's Jury was unable to fathom how anyone could have entered the compartment of a moving train and killed Miss Crawford, so they gave up and brought in a verdict of accidental death.

There the matter rests to this day. It might have been totally forgotten if a report in the *Birmingham Post* of 6th December 1890 had not come under the eye of an American called Charles Forte. Forte was an assiduous collector of anomalies, of reports of events that made no apparent sense. He published four wonderful collections of strange stories to which he added his comments, *The Book of the Damned, New Lands, Lo!* and *Wild Talents*. In America and Britain there are societies that keep his name and his work alive. Here we have the monthly magazine *Fortean Times* which collects and publishes similarly strange stories, and publishes Charles Forte's four books.

In *Wild Talents* he tells the story of Matilda Crawford and her invisible murderer and offers an explanation. Now, one needs to be a little cautious with Forte. He was very often sarcastic and put forward bizarre explanations by way of comment on the grotesque attempts of scientists to explain away unusual phenomena. So perhaps he was not serious when he suggested the existence of a young man somewhere in the Midlands, tormented by a deep desire to molest women on trains. This young man's obsession became so powerful that a thought created image of himself went off to find a victim, and was drawn to Matilda, alone in her compartment and dwelling on the then frequent stories of misconduct by males in railway compartments.

Well, it is an explanation, if not a terribly satisfactory or believable one. Is any other explanation possible? It is easy to say that the killer must have been the detective, but it is very unlikely. He would have to have been fool- hardy and skilful enough to climb out of a moving train, edge along its narrow footboard and open the door of another compartment to climb in. Nothing Miss Crawford said indicated that the killer entered while the train was moving. Anyway, if he had done so the detective would surely have covered his crime by describing a fictitious man entering the compartment?

So what did happen? Was she pushed, or did she fall? Did she believe that the train would stop at Soho and attempt to get off? Her ticket was for Snow Hill. Was she desperate to use a toilet by the time the train reached Soho? Did she mistake Soho for Snow Hill and believe she was being carried past her destination?

Certainly, if she attempted to open the door of the compartment she might well have tumbled out. Carriage doors then as now, had no inside handles. To open a door from the inside you had to drop the window, lean right out and use the outside handle. Easy to tumble out if you were not very large, even easier if the train rocked on the rails while you were doing it.

So, perhaps she fell, but if she did, why did she tell the story of the murderously lustful young man? Maybe Forte is right there. Perhaps she was not an experienced traveller by rail or perhaps she was constitutionally nervous. Finding herself alone in a non corridor compartment, perhaps she dwelt on the frequent horror stories of lone women being molested by male passengers in such compartments.

This is not the place to tell the whole astonishing story of Colonel Valentine Baker, but his case rocked Victorian England and had results which may bear on Miss Crawford's death. In June 1874 a young woman was seen hanging from the door of a train approaching Esher in Surrey. When the train stopped there the girl, a Miss Rebecca Kate Dickinson of Midhurst, accused a fellow passenger in her First Class compartment of 'insulting her' and refusing to 'leave her alone'.

Her fellow traveller was 49 year old Colonel Valentine Baker, Assistant Quartermaster General at Aldershot, a friend of the Prince of Wales and of the Duke of Cambridge, the Commander in Chief of the British Army. Nevertheless, three days later, he was arrested and Guildford Magistrates subsequently committed him for trial for indecent assault and 'assault with intent to ravish'.

Found guilty of indecent assault only, Baker was sentenced to twelve months' in gaol and cashiered from the Army. Emerging from prison, the Colonel took his wife and family abroad where he became 'Baker Pasha', the first Lieutenant General in the Ottoman Army and later Commander of the Egyptian gendarmerie under the Khedive. When he returned to Britain for a period of convalescence after being wounded, a cheering crowd greeted him at Victoria Station. He died in 1887 and was buried, by the Commander in Chief's specific order, with full military honours and four British generals in attendance.

Giles Playfair discusses the case in *A Clutch of Curious Characters,* (Xanadu, 1984 ed. Richard Glyn Jones) suggesting that Miss Dickinson was less innocent than she seemed and drawing attention to the fact that it was she who prosecuted Colonel Baker, not the Police. He concludes:

> "Even the idea, still much cherished, that a sensationalised trial serves a useful deterrent purpose turned out to be a palpable pretence on this occasion. For the case was followed by a veritable outbreak of indecent assaults in railway carriages. Colonel Baker's lasting monument is the corridor."

A veritable outbreak of indecent assaults for Miss Crawford to dwell on nervously in her lonely compartment? When some accident threw her from the train, injuring her so seriously that she died within hours, was her damaged brain filled with the images that had occupied it on the journey? Was what she told the Police merely the fantasy of a Victorian girl frightened by stories like that of Colonel Baker and his host of imitators? Was the detective so unobservant that he missed a man getting into the compartment? Or was Matilda Crawford killed by an invisible murderer?

This Great Western railway line was taken up years ago but the trackbed is now used for the new Birmingham - Wolver hampton tramway.

'You have murdered me.'
(Ranton, Staffs 1833)

'Blood will out', the sanctimonious say with satisfaction when
the son or daughter of a miscreant witnesses their ancestry by
misbehaving. They seem to forget that more kindly proverb:
'Give a dog a bad name and hang him'.

Richard Tomlinson was given a bad name and it hanged him.
His start in life might have been envied by many in the early
19th century. His parents were able to leave him an inheritance
of £250 when both died within a short time of each other. It was
not the fact of their deaths but the manner of them that branded
Richard, and brought about his own end.

Richard was born in Ranton village, near Stafford, and was only
eleven years old when his father, John Tomlinson, died suddenly
after a short illness. Local gossip suggested poison, and after
exhumation a post mortem revealed a large amount of arsenic
in the late Mr Tomlinson.

Arsenic was a common chemical in those days, used in industrial
processes, sheep dips, paint and printers' ink, rat poison and many
common items. Accidental arsenic poisoning was frequent. Even so,
Richard's mother was taken up on suspicion and lodged in Stafford
Gaol. The rumour was that she had poisoned her husband's porridge
and given it to little Richard to deliver to his father.

What a child psychologist would make of that situation we do not
know. Nor do we know if the story was more than rumour. Richard's
mother was robbed of her day in Court, and perhaps, her day on the
gallows, when she died in prison before her trial.

The orphan Richard was raised by relatives and eventually enlisted
in the Royal Marines. Ranton probably expected to see him only
years later, sunburned from defending the Empire, or perhaps not
at all. In the event, he was back at the age of 21, discharged
from the Royal Marines as 'unsuited to military discipline'.

He had come home to collect his inheritance and, with the
money safely in hand, he passed the time in his brother in
law's beerhouse or in courting Mary Evans, described as,
'a very interesting and amiable young woman'.

Ranton Church

Mary's father was Joseph Evans, Parish Clerk, and in those days such officials were more important (and more self important) than they are today. Joseph would not see his daughter married to a dissolute ex Marine, whose idea of fun was to fling explosives into a beerhouse fire, and whose mother had died in prison under taint of poisoning.

If Richard and Mary could not marry because of Joseph's objections, they did nor deprive themselves of the pleasures of matrimony. Mary's sister lived in a cottage at nearby Knightly where they spent nights in bed, Mary wearing a ring to salve her sister's conscience. They also took a fair share of the difficulties of marriage because their relationship readily flared into argument.

A row burst over them on Monday 16th December 1833 after they had spent the weekend at Knightley. Mary accused Richard of stealing from her. He denied it. She decided to consult a 'cunning man', a clairvoyant or conjurer, in High Ercall and set off there with Richard and her brother in law, John Dabbs. Richard turned back after a mile or two claiming to be ill.

What Mr Light, the cunning man said, we do not know, but on the way back to Knightley John Dabbs warned Mary to be careful of Richard. From Knightley, Richard and Mary set out for Ranton and as they walked the row exploded again.

They were by Ranton church when Mary flung yet another heated insult at Richard. She sneered at him as the son of a mother who had died in prison after poisoning his father. He was outraged and demanded that she withdraw the slur. She refused and he knocked her down, apparently with a big stone.

Again he demanded a withdrawal and once more she refused. Sprawled on the ground she shrieked, "You have murdered me!" Richard sprang on her back shouting, 'If I've not I will die', and forced her face into the December mud.

Afterwards Richard said he remembered nothing until he found that Mary was dead. Leaving her in a ditch, he made his way to a pub and joined a farmer called Betteley. They were drinking together when Mary's body was discovered, and Richard was asking Betteley if he had actually seen him kill Mary when a Constable arrived to arrest him.

His trial at Stafford was a formality. The best the defence could put forward was Richard's habit of alarming drinkers at the beerhouse by flinging gunpowder on the fire. This was not, they argued, 'the act of a normal man'. They might have argued that a youth who was too unruly for the discipline of the Royal Marines at that time could hardly have been normal.

Today he could argue for a manslaughter verdict on the basis of provocation, but in 1833 the inevitable verdict was guilty of murder.

Richard Tomlinson was executed at Stafford on 17th March 1834. It was a triple bill shared with 16 year old Charles Shaw, who had strangled a 9 year old workmate at the Etruria Pottery, and Mary Smith who had drowned her baby in the canal at Bloxwich.

'The brightest child of God.'
(Leicester 1832)

Mr Paas of High Holborn, London, was a brass founder.
Amongst other items he supplied the tools used by book
binders to apply the gold leaf ornament to titles or covers.
In the early summer of 1832 he set out on a journey around
certain customers at a distance from London. They all owed
him money and he had written to each one to say that he would
be calling for settlement.

Among the debtors was James Cook, a book binder of
Wellington Street, Leicester. Master of his own business
at twenty two, Cook had had a lucky start in life. A stout
youth of medium height and not, it seems, very clever, he had
nevertheless been such a dutiful apprentice that his master, on
dying, had left him the business. As an apprentice he had enjoyed
not only the approval of his employer, but also a reputation as a
good young man. As a skilled craftsman, secure in the possession
of his own business at an early age, the future looked bright for
young Cook.

Maybe his late master possessed qualities of leadership or
instruction that brought out the best in Cook, but after taking
over the workshop he became lazy. Working only when he felt
like it, he alienated good customers and sank rapidly into
debt so that bankruptcy seemed inevitable.

In those circumstances you might think that a letter from Mr Paas
announcing his forthcoming visit would be just another burden to
the hard pressed Cook, but he saw it as an opportunity. For some
time he had been thinking that emigration and a fresh start else-
where was his only hope, but emigration required passage
money and funds to start again, which he did not have.

It occurred to Cook that if Mr Paas had collected from a number
of other debtors before calling at Wellington Street, he would be
carrying enough cash to solve all Cook's problems. He began to
plan, if the steps he took can be dignified by that term. First he
lit an abnormally large fire in his workshop on the evening of
29th May 1832 and left it burning when he locked up. A neighbour complained of the risk that the fire might destroy the street,
but Cook told him, "The furnace is properly safe. I banked it up
myself. I am very busy just now and I may have to work late
tomorrow night".

Satisfied that he had laid the grounds of his plot, he welomed Mr
Paas into his workshop the next evening and sent his boy out on a
pointless errand, telling him not to return till morning. Paas was
bigger than Cook, but of course, suspected nothing. Cook agreed
to pay him, and as Paas bent over the table to write out a receipt
Cook struck him dead with a blow to the back of the head.

His expectations were rewarded with £60 in cash plus a watch,
rings and other jewellery, but he had now to dispose of the body.
Should you take to murder do be warned, the greatest difficulty
that a murderer faces is disposal of the body, and burning is not
a good way. The average human being contains about six litres of
water and will not burn well, as Cook discovered. He worked for
hours to dispose of Mr Paas, harder than he had worked since his
apprenticeship, but by 9 o'clock he was exhausted. He went home
but could not sleep. At 1 o'clock in the morning he returned to
the workshop and continued his efforts, telling his family that
he had to complete an important order.

Throughout the next day he kept his furnace high, causing comment
in passers by, who saw the flames lighting his window blinds and
wondered at the sudden industry of this idle young man. Late in
the evening he took a break at the Flying Horse inn, where he paid
for his food and ale from a fistful of gold and silver and played
a game of skittles before going home to bed.

He was roused at 11 o'clock by a party of men. They said that the
landlord of the Flying Horse, frightened by the continuing fire in
Cook's premises, had broken into the workshop and found something suspicious.

At the scene of the murder, Cook was confronted by a Constable
Measures, who seems to have been the worse for drink. He asked
Cook to account for a quantity of smouldering flesh and Cook
replied that it was horseflesh. This so confused Constable Measures that he agreed to take a surety for Cook until a doctor could
examine the evidence. Cook's father stood bail for him, whereupon
he returned to his father's cottage, packed a few belongings and
left by the back door to catch the Liverpool coach.

On the following day a doctor proclaimed the remains in the
workshop to be human flesh and the hue and cry began. Cook
was unlucky in that he arrived at Liverpool to find no American
boat sailing for some days. He lay low, but in the meantime the
authorities traced him to Liverpool. When an American bound
vessel was due to depart, Cook dared not board at the landing,
but bribed a boatman to take him out to join the ship in the

river. In a scene worthy of any 19th century melodrama, he was
rowed into the Mersey only to find his boat pursued by a boatful
of constables. In despair he produced a bottle of laudanum and
was about to swallow a fatal dose when his pursuers reached
him and saved him for Leicester Assize.

Lodged in gaol, Cook became a celebrity. His brutal crime and
dramatic flight had made him national news. Tourists came to the
prison and bribed several guards to let them see and talk to the
murderer. Cook accepted their adulation and insisted that he had
killed Paas by accident during a quarrel. He explained that he had
felt obliged to destroy the body because no one would believe him,
an excuse that even then was centuries old.

Contemporary woodcut

Among those who read of and were interested in Cook's plight
was the daughter of a wealthy family in Northampton, the Paynes
of Sulby Manor. Miss Payne was recovering from an illness
and searching, perhaps subconsciously, for means to while away
the dull existence of a respectable single lady. She came upon
the idle little thug from Leicester and conceived the notion
that it was her mission in life to convert this unprepossessing
oaf and save his soul.

Miss Payne was supported and helped in her bizarre campaign by a friend, Mrs Lachlan. Mrs Lachlan was no invalid, she was in every way what used to be called a muscular Christian. She was also a prolific writer whose first work, *The Twins of Chamouni*, had been 'dedicated by special permission of the Duchess of Kent to HRH the Princess Victoria', when the Princess was thirteen.

What cynical modern minds might make of the relationship between the young Miss Payne and her older friend, a lady who dedicated her first book to a young girl, is immaterial. It is quite clear that the only passion which they shared was for religion, with a capital R, and for dragging the sinful under its umbrella. How they went about this in the case of James Cook was recorded by Mrs Lachlan herself in a remarkable work called *Narrative of the Conversion (by the instrumentality of Two Ladies) of James Cook, The Murderer of Mr Paas, in Letters Addressed to a Clergyman of the Established Church.*

Miss Payne opened the campaign by writing to Cook telling him that repentance would send him straight from the gallows to Heaven. Dull he might have been, but not too stupid to reject the friendship of the wealthy. He invited her to visit him and a few days later the 'Two Ladies' arrived at the gaol with a basket of fruit, a dozen cambric handkerchiefs and sundry other little comforts and, inevitably, a handsomely bound bible.

At first Cook played hard to get, seeming to be the heartless ruffian that he was, but knowing that this would only whet Miss Payne's enthusiasm. Eventually however he 'succumbed' to her entreaties and confessed. This was a worthless gesture in worldly terms, since his defence was laughable and the evidence against him massive, but the act stirred Miss Payne to raptures. She wrote to Mrs Lachlan:

"He is ripening so fast for Heaven, that such a sight I never could have imagined I should behold on earth. Could you but see him! He takes the Bible and astonishes us with his beautiful childlike remarks. He does indeed answer the description of receiving the kingdom of God as a little child. In fact, words can never give you an idea of the amazing wonderful change in this being. Christ shines in every look and every word. He seems to feel that God sent us to him, and says he longed to make a full confession to us the first day we saw him,

but that the devil prevented him, and that what we had
said had such an effect on him, that he never rested
till he had confessed. His ripening for Heaven is the
most rapid and wonderful thing I ever beheld. He is
the brightest child of God I ever saw."

And so on and so on, with a few lines later a hint of New Age
confusion which is not new. The impressionable have always liked
to construct themselves a dramatic philosophy from what scraps of
religion, philosophy, folklore and science appeal to their jackdaw
minds:

"The nearness of the Comet, too, which is expected
next October, calls for our serious attention. The
world is to be burnt up, and I think it will be at
that time. What bliss, to be changed in the twinkling
of an eye, and be for ever with the Lord!"

Within the prison, the 'brightest child of God' was a celebrity
and a power. A constant flow of wine, food, linen and money
came from his converter and no doubt some was dispensed in
obtaining other comforts. Sometimes the Gaoler and his whole
family would attend 'services' held by Cook, lustily singing
hymns while watchers exclaimed at the charity and goodness
of the erstwhile bookbinder.

The prison Chaplain tried to stop Miss Payne's visits, but Cook
prayed at him and forgave him. "I will forgive my enemies ten
times seventy times seven", he said on one occasion. "I am not
sorry for myself, only for the millions who are not converted, for
I am going to heaven and they are going to hell." A curious form
of Godliness you might think, that allows a man to beat a stranger
to death for money, run away from the consequences, lie about it
when caught, then change his mind and pass from the gallows to
heaven. In the meantime innocent, truthful millions are condemned
to hellfire because they lived without benefit of Miss Payne.

Cook eventually appeared before Mr Justice Park who cannot
have been ignorant of the fantastic goings on in Leicester Gaol.
The press had made several scornful references to them. He seemed
not to believe in Cook's conversion because when Cook had pleaded
guilty to murder, the Judge exhorted him to turn from his wicked-
ness and seek forgiveness - Above.

Observers believed that once sentenced to death Cook's hypo-
critical mask cracked as he was led back to his cell, and an
expression of terror appeared. Certainly it cracked in the cell,
where his old loutish personality reappeared and he collapsed
cursing. Even so, he was soon telling a warder that, "I hope
poor Mr Paas has forgiven me, otherwise it will be so awkward
for both of us when we meet in heaven."

So he rose heavenwards at least as high as the noose, and *The Age*
newspaper commented:

> "A more hardhearted and depraved ruffian never dropped
> from a gallows - and the penny a line men report him, of
> course, as dying firm, undaunted, heroic, etc, etc. The
> greater the scoundrel, the greater the favourite with them
>   ..... we shall not quarrel with them through endeav-
> ouring to obtain the price of an extra pint of beer by a
> few extra lines; but there is something to us infinitely
> disgusting in the interference of some Leicester women,
> particularly a Miss Payne, in the case. What have women
> to do with a beastly murderer who was not a degree above
> the New Zealanders? Some snuffling saint will answer,
> she was impelled by piety.
>
> Stuff! Had he not spiritual advice enough without her
> volunteer assistance? She might have left the business
> to the chaplain. This vagabond, on his trial, never took
> his eyes off a book he was reading but once, and that
> was to ogle Miss Payne who sat on the bench and on his
> leaving the dock he kissed his hands to her. We suppose
> she had a lock of his hair as a memento. It was on the
> whole a most disgusting exhibition of cant and
> hypocrisy."

Apart from the Maoris of New Zealand, most people would have
applauded the sentiments expressed by *The Age*. However, James
Cook was not done with disgusting exhibitions. At that time it was
official policy to gibbet murderers, that is, to coat their corpses
in pitch as a preservative and hang them in chains or iron cages
at road junctions as a warning to potential imitators.

Cook was gibbeted at Saffron Lane. His dangling remains
drew a crowd of revellers estimated at twenty thousand, who
were supplied by stalls selling food and drink. The drunken
celebration of Cook's execution continued until a massive
rainstorm swept the area. All night Cook's corpse swung in

the howling winds and beating rain as the last revellers trudged home. Miss Payne and Mrs Lachlan would probably have regarded the weather's manifestation as the Lord's punishment on the drunken revellers. The revellers fled, probably believing that Satan had come to take his own.

The government took a third view. It decided that if gibbeting was going to attract drunken multitudes, they would end the practice. Modern commentators have suggested that the change was made for reasons of humanity and decency. It was not; it was just another swerve in the onward march of 'law and order'.

The Comet came and went without burning up the world and, so far as we know, Miss Payne survived, no doubt adjusting her beliefs accordingly. Wherever Cook's soul had gone, his mortal remains rotted away on England's last active gibbet.

'Help! They have got me.'
(Colonne, Belgium 1940)

The ordinary jurisdiction of a Magistrates' Court, or Court of Petty Session, covers an area known as a Petty Sessional Division. All crimes charged within that Division must come before the local Magistrates' Court, even if they are ultimately to be tried in the Crown Court.

The Birmingham Petty Sessional Division is a large one, justifying Brummies in building the Victoria Law Courts, possibly the most splendid of Magistrates' Court buildings. Most Magistrates' Courts are fully occupied with their local supply of crime and have no need to seek cases from outside the Division, but in 1946 a Birmingham Stipendiary Magistrate found himself hearing a case which had originated nearly six years previously in Belgium. It was the first time that Birmingham had tried a case arising abroad, murder being one of the few crimes where the power exists, provided the accused is a British citizen and within the Court's jurisdiction.

World War Two in Europe had ended in the summer of 1945. Home came not only soldiers, sailors and airmen but also many prisoners released from German prison camps. For those captured early in the fighting it had been a long wait, but at last they were home and demobbed and most of them could put the war behind them.

Not all of them. Back to Handsworth, Birmingham, came a Corporal Mavity, formerly of the Royal Warwickshire Regiment. As Christmas 1945 approached he was arrested by Inspector Foreman of Birmingham CID and Detective Inspector Burney from Scotland Yard who charged him with murdering his company commander, Captain Guy Glover, on 20th May 1940 at Colonne, near Tournai in Belgium.

When Mavity appeared in Birmingham Magistrates' Court the Prosecutor was Mervyn Phippen Pugh, the City's Prosecuting Solicitor since 1924, and who continued until 1958. Opening the case, he said:

> "I will call evidence to prove that Mavity and Glover had been in the same Company since 1929. In January 1940 the 8th Battalion went to France, and just prior to that the accused had been promoted to lance sergeant. He was, however reduced to corporal when disciplinary action was taken against him. A witness whom I shall call noticed this and questioned Mavity about it, and his reply was: 'That ******* got me this for being drunk. He needn't think he's going to get away with it. I shall certainly get him when he gets up the line.
>
> If you believe that Mavity did make that threatening statement, it will help you to form an opinion as to why he eventually did fire a shot from the effects of which Captain Glover died."

Mr Pugh seems to have ignored the fact that abusing their officers is a long standing practice of soldiers and does not usually end in murder.

Pugh admitted that he was in difficulty, even about the time of Glover's death. Glover's unit had been engaged in a fighting retreat for a week. They were exhausted, without food, and under intermittent shelling, mortar and rifle fire. A number of witnesses to Glover's death had been killed later and some were suffering from the strain of battle. Pugh put the incident at about 9.30 p.m. on the evening of 20th May 1940.

> "Witnesses will say that Captain Glover received a message from a runner and left company headquarters. Shortly afterwards a rifle shot was heard nearby, and a witness will say he heard Captain Glover shout, 'Help! They have got me!'."

Nobody had seen the shot fired. Corporal Gough heard the shot and found Captain Glover on the ground wounded in the upper chest. He was losing consciousness and said that he had been shot but not who had shot him. The Captain's last words were to ask for his mother.

The unit's Medical Officer, Captain N S Robinson attended Glover saying, 'Why did they have to do this to you? I'll put you out of your misery. There's no hope for you'. Then he administered an injection and Captain Glover died without regaining consciousness. He was buried near the Company Headquarters.

The press were rightly concerned about Captain Robinson's part in the affair. The *Daily Mail* found former officers of the Royal Warwicks who told them that Glover and Robinson were like brothers. Within a few days of Glover's death Robinson was killed in action while tending wounded. They added that when the battalion had first gone overseas officer friends of Captain Robinson said to him, "If anything happens to us, deal with us, Robbie, won't you?"

After the shot Mavity appeared at company headquarters, saying, 'I've come to report I've shot Captain Glover as a spy. You're all ******* spies'. He raised his rifle and was told by Captain Sparrow to drop it. There was a struggle in which Mavity was struck in the mouth with a rifle butt, then he was restrained and sent under escort to Headquarters. His rifle was examined and an empty cartridge found in the breech. On the way to head-quarters Mavity kept repeating, 'I want a fair trial' and said 'I saw tanks up the road and I told Lieutenant Potts but he wouldn't take any notice of me. They are all spies'. One witness reported that Mavity 'appeared to have gone off his head and his eyes were glaring'.

On the following day, Pugh told the Court, the Germans over-ran the village, Mavity was captured and that was an end of the matter until the war ended. Back in Handsworth on 4th December 1945 he said to the two detectives who arrested him, 'I guessed what it is all about'. When charged he added, 'I remember shooting him, but my mind was a blank at the time. I would like to tell you. It has worried me ever since'.

He made a statement telling how he had joined the Territorial Army, had met Captain Glover and eventually gone to France.

In May 1940 the regiment had moved to the Belgian frontier.
Mavity had been tired and ill and kept seeing things. He
also 'felt' that Captain Glover was a spy.

> " ... I saw him coming towards me from just behind the firing
> line. I asked him why the messenger sent by me to HQ had not
> returned. He turned around and then went back to HQ and then
> he came back carrying his revolver. I thought he was going to
> shoot me with his revolver. I had my rifle with me with one
> bullet up the spout. I put my rifle to my shoulder and shot
> him."

Mavity had said that he had no grievance against his commander,
but,

> "I really thought he was a spy at the time because the mess-
> enger had not returned to me. I still think I must have been
> off my head when I did it. I never made any secret of the
> incident and told some of my men about it".

Mr Pugh pretended to assist the defence,

> "I intend to put in everything relating to the prisoner's
> state of mind at the time of the alleged shooting so that the
> defence can make the fullest possible use of it'.

This came after he had suggested that the shooting was a
premeditated act of revenge. Pugh went on to say that there
was not a scintilla of evidence that Captain Glover was a
spy, that he had been greatly loved and respected and was
a true British patriot.

Mavity was defended by Harry Faber, possibly the best known
of Birmingham's criminal solicitors. At this point he intervened
to say that he had received no instructions from Mavity which
suggested that Glover was not a British officer of the highest
character.

Pugh returned to his attempts to prove premeditation when he
called evidence. However, an ex Company Sergeant Major of
the Warwickshire Regiment would not confirm that Mavity's
threat over his loss of promotion was serious, pointing out
that it did not even involve loss of pay. 'Come, come, you
are a soldier', urged Pugh, striving for evidence of resentment. 'I'm not', said the witness. 'I'm a civilian'.

Witnesses described how Mavity and his company had been fighting and marching for seven days and had not slept for three. When arrested Mavity had struggled against being placed in a cellar, saying 'Don't put me down there. There's gas down there. I know you're going to kill me. Shoot me!' He was shut in a schoolroom, where he had to be bound hand and foot. During heavy shelling that night he had told his guards that they were all in Heaven and he would take care of them.

The unit's only surviving officer told how he held a Court of Inquiry before which Mavity appeared charged with murder. The Medical Officer, the late Captain Robinson, had declared that Mavity was insane and, as a result the Brigadier cancelled his order for a Field General Court Martial.

At the close of the Prosecution evidence, Harry Faber submitted that this was not a matter where a man should be committed to stand trial risking the death penalty.

"Is there any evidence before the Court to show the shot he fired killed this man, or any evidence to show the shot fired caused the death? Not one witness can say, 'I saw this man shoot Captain Glover.' All they can say is, 'We heard a shot.'

"But Mavity has admitted the shooting', said the Stipendiary Magistrate, Lord Ilkeston. Faber replied:

"He may think he did, but there is no evidence to show the shot he fired caused Captain Glover's death."

These were committal proceedings, and the Stipendiary's duty was to consider whether the Prosecution had shown sufficient evidence to obtain a conviction if the matter was committed to a superior court, then the Assizes.

In fact, Mr Pugh had been in difficulties from the start. Not only had he not been able to substantiate revenge for demotion as motive for a premeditated murder, he had no witness to the shooting. The one witness who heard the shot said that Glover cried out that 'they' had got him. What is more, even if it was Mavity's shot that wounded Glover, there was no evidence that it had killed him. That evidence could only have come from the late Captain Robinson, whose own part in Captain Glover's death was equivocal. There was even, in Mavity's statement to the

Police a suggestion of self defence if he had genuinely believed that Glover was about to kill him. Such a belief does not have to reasonable.

The military Court of Inquiry had found Mavity insane on the evidence of the Medical Officer, who knew him and knew his experiences of the previous week, so that there had been no Court Martial. Had Birmingham Magistrates' Court refused to commit the case for trial the matter would have ended there, unless the Prosecutor could find new evidence. But Birmingham Magistrates' Court was entitled, quite unfairly, to ignore the decision of the Court of Inquiry.

None of the evidence and the obvious conclusions bothered Lord Ilkeston. Relying on the admissions of a man who had been judged insane at the relevant time, he committed Mavity to the Assizes to stand trial for capital murder.

The Committal placed Harry Faber in a desperately awkward predicament. Weak as the case against Mavity was, the Stipendiary had committed for trial and if Mavity pleaded not guilty at the Assize a Jury might still find him guilty. In that case the death sentence was inevitable.

When the case came before Birmingham Assize in March 1946 Mavity pleaded 'guilty but insane', and was ordered to be detained in a hospital for criminal lunatics. His statement to the Police does not suggest that he was insane in 1945, and the plea only meant that he was insane at the time of Captain Glover's death. Someone, somewhere, had succeeded in making the point that soldiers may not shoot their officers and get away with it.

If someone was insane when they killed someone they were out of their mind, so how can they be 'guilty' of a crime? The very nature of the defence is that they were so confused that they did not know what they were doing. The story is that a man took a shot at Queen Victoria and was found not guilty of attempted murder, or whatever he was charged with, because he was insane. The Queen was greatly offended by the idea that a person should not be guilty of something or other for shooting at her, so the form of the the plea was changed.

The case leaves many unanswered questions, not least a speculation as to whose interest was served by bringing Mavity to trial. The Army seems to have washed its hands of him by holding an inquiry, finding him insane and refusing to put him before a Court Martial.

Was there really such an inquiry? Did this hard pressed, exhausted unit, on the verge of being overrun by the enemy really take the time to hold a formal inquiry, for which the Regulations required at least two officers to hear formal evidence, write it down, and a make a written report to the Brigadier? Little wonder that the Germans captured the unit if their officers were busy discussing the sanity of Corporal Mavity.

Military proceedings against Mavity could only take place within five years of the incident. By December 1945 they were barred by the Army Act of 1861. Did the Army wish to proceed and, prevented by the Army Act, pretend that it had held a military inquiry in 1940 and leave him to the civil power? Had the Army really finished with him? Was his trial in 1946 the result of someone else's initiative?

'It was her fault.'
(Oldbury, Worcs 1913)

Emigration to America was always a way out of the poverty and grime of England's industrial cities. Twenty one year old Thomas Fletcher was one of many who dreamed of escape in the early years of the 20th century. One of the two sons and six daughters of a widowed mother who crowded into a tiny house at 17, Dudley Road, he worked as a railway shunter in Oldbury. Tom had good reason to get away if he could. He must have thought that he had achieved his dream and all who knew him must have envied his luck when, in 1906 with his brother William, he sailed to join relatives already settled in Virginia.

Tom's luck was really in, and once across the water everything worked out exactly as he had hoped. He and his brother became gold prospectors and shared excellent profits. Young Tom spent his money freely, dressed sharply and quickly picked up the accent of his adopted country. But for a twist of fate he might never have returned to Britain.

William Fletcher fell ill in 1911, so seriously it seems that the brothers decided to return to Oldbury, either because Bill's illness was terminal or because they put more faith in English doctors. Whatever Bill's intentions, Tom certainly meant to treat the trip as a visit and return to America. In the autumn of 1911 they embarked at New York, but Bill was so sick that he had to be removed from the ship and travelled later.

Almost all of Tom's family except his mother travelled to Birmingham's New Street Station to welcome him, and they packed a tram as they escorted him home. In 1987 his great niece, Mrs Bird, remembered the return of her handsome great uncle. "He was a great favourite with all the family, and a real gentleman. Of course, he had acquired some wealth in America and brought back many expensive items of jewellery."

The good looking, well dressed young man soon became widely recognised in and around Oldbury, where his distinctive accent led to him being nicknamed 'The American'. He spent his transatlantic wealth carelessly in pubs, where he readily recounted his adventures on the other side of the 'herring pond'. He must have been a magnet for unmarried girls, many of whom shared the dream of emigration, and he soon formed the intention of acquiring a wife from his home town and taking her back to America.

Unfortunately Tom's free and easy lifestyle depleted his funds to the point where he could no longer afford his own ticket back to the States, let alone that of a wife or the cost of setting up home.

He took a job as a labourer at Hughes & Johnson's stamping works in Langley, intending to save up for a wife and passage to America. Soon he had engaged the affections of Lilian Wharton, twenty one year old daughter of the landlord at the Fountain Inn in Albion Street, Brades Village. Once again it seemed that Tom's luck was rolling.

Through the winter of 1912 the young couple were making plans to marry on 26th March 1913. The banns were posted at Dudley Registry Office and everything seemed to be going smoothly.

Then Tom lost his job. It was a perfect excuse for Lilian's father, a hardworking employee of Withers Safe Works in West Bromwich, to forbid the marriage, and one which he seized on. He did not like Tom Fletcher's lifestyle and didn't regard him as a suitable son in law.

John Wharton told young Fletcher that he was not well enough off to marry Lilian. Tom was furious and humiliated. Having returned triumphantly rich from America he was now spurned as a suitor through poverty. Lilian was upset but strove to fall in with her father's wishes. She tried to persuade Tom to wait until he could acquire enough money to satisfy her father and marry her. It did not work. As the days moved on towards their cancelled wedding date, Tom became more morose and irritable.

On 26th March, the planned wedding day, Tom and Lilian met at the Fountain. An argument developed and he was heard to threaten her. She told her mother of his threat and Mrs Wharton tried to calm him down, telling him that, 'A woman needs good pluck to go to church with a man who threatens her'. Tom refused to discuss the matter with Mrs Wharton, and she suggested that he stay away from Lilian for four or five weeks, until he calmed down.

He stayed away for five days. On the third day he visited Holland's pawnshop in King Street, Dudley, where he gave a false address and bought a revolver for 10/6d (52 1/2p). George Jennings, the shop assistant, accepted Tom's peculiar reason, that he needed it to protect himself in his own home and let him have the weapon. At Griffiths's gunshop in Stone Street he purchased cartridges.

At about 10.30 on the morning of 1st April Tom appeared at the Fountain, bought a brandy and chatted to Lilian, while her mother withdrew to feed the chickens so as not to play goose-berry. Moments later she heard several reports of a gun from inside the pub, and screams. She dashed back into the bar to see her daughter clutching her side and screaming, "Tom has shot me!".

Lilian went out onto the pavement, her mother followed and noted on the way that Tom Fletcher lay on the tap room floor with blood pouring from his head.

Lilian's cries brought neighbours running. Rebecca Hall, who could see no injury, told her, "No, you're not shot", but the injured girl collapsed into the arms of Lilian Shakespeare and was carried to a sofa in the back of the pub. Police and a doctor were summoned and Inspector Price arrived with Sergeant Wall and Dr Cooke.

Nowadays radio and television bring us even the local news, but word of mouth spread the news of the shooting at Albion Street. Tom's mother was on her way to Oldbury when she heard a roadsweeper at Clayton's Bridge shouting to some boatmen, "Tom Fletcher has shot Lily at the Fountain!". She fell in a faint.

Tom's brother in law, Sam Hall, was in the barber's chair being shaved when the news was brought into the shop. Wiping the lather from his face, he ran to the Fountain.

Tom and Lilian were rushed to West Bromwich District Hospital where Tom's condition was thought to be the worse. Mr F Keane, the surgeon, described Tom's injury as a deep bullet graze on the right temple. Lilian had a bullet wound in the left side, two inches below the ribs, and a septic graze on the right index finger.

Sergeant Price sat by Fletcher's bed until he recovered consciousness and recorded that the young man had said, "I suppose I shall have to go through it for this when I get better. I have not killed her, it was her fault. I only fired two shots at her. I wish I had killed myself".

Lilian appeared to be making a good recovery, but after several days she relapsed and on 8th April, died. A post mortem examination showed a bullet lodged in the intestines which had set up a fatal inflammation of the abdomen. Tom Fletcher was charged with murder.

Coroner Clark opened an Inquest on Lilian at West Bromwich Law Courts on 11th April but then adjourned to allow time for Tom to recover and leave hospital. On 26th April Oldbury Police Court heard evidence, including Tom's explanation that his sole intention had been to shoot himself and that Lilian had been accidentally shot when she tried to stop him. But perhaps the remark, "I only fired two shots at her" was conclusive. He was committed for trial at Worcester Assizes, a decision confirmed two days later by the Coroner's Court.

Sympathy for Tom Fletcher ran high in Oldbury. Many people were prepared to believe his version of events and a public subscription was raised to pay for his defence. Even so, on 7th June the jury at Worcester Assize found him guilty and Mr Justice Bray sentenced him to hang.

His large family packed the public benches in Worcester's Shire Hall as once they had packed a tram when they welcomed him home. Hysterical cries greeted the sentence, his sister Catherine Turley calling out, "Oh! My poor brother!". Tom Fletcher called to them, "All of you look after mother, and tell her to give young Sammy (his nephew) my gold watch and chain".

Public sympathy stayed with him. When the Court of Appeal rejected an application for an appeal a petition to the Home Secretary for clemency was organised, but that too was rejected.

Tom Fletcher's luck had turned bad when he lost his job, worse when his marriage plans ended, and worse still when Surgeon Keane's team failed to find the second bullet in Lilian. X-ray photographs were available then, and expert probing of the wound was already established procedure in gunshot cases. Either would have revealed the bullet and probably allowed Lilian to recover. Tom would have been charged with attempted murder at the worst.

His luck finally ran out with the Home Secretary's rejection of the petition. On Wednesday 9th July 1913 he was hanged in Worcester Prison. Little Sammy never got the gold watch and chain because the family couldn't find it.

Still standing

'Another glass or two of brandy.'
(Oddingley, Worcs 1806)

'Nothing', they say, 'is as sure as death and taxes'. This story starts with taxes and ends with deaths.

The scene of the crimes was Oddingley, a village near Droitwich. You might not think this is the sort of place for multiple murder, except perhaps in a Miss Marple story. Sherlock Holmes, on the other hand, despite his wide experience of city crime, cast a jaundiced eye on the countryside.

> "You look at these scattered houses' he told Watson,' and you are impressed by their beauty. I look at them, and the only thought which comes to me is a feeling of their isolation, and of the impunity with which crime may be committed there."

The first murder was brought about by greed, the greed of the Vicar of Oddingley. For eight centuries vicars of Church of England parishes were entitled to levy a tax of 10% on the annual produce of local landowners, the 'tithe'. This was so even if those taxed didn't attended the church or even went to a non conformist chapel. Nothing since they gave up burning heretics brought the established Church into more odium. Many vicars were men of independent income who could well afford to ignore or reduce the tithe, and did so. Others, just as wealthy, insisted on their last penny and sometimes more. By the mid 19th century the issue had split many parishes, the more so since many tithe grabbing vicars were of a High Church persuasion and introduced practices and forms of service that many parishioners thought idolatrous and blasphemous.

At Sedgeley near Dudley in 1862 a disgruntled landowner published a book, attacking the Reverend William Lewis, *A Round Unvarnished Tale of the Exploits of the Vicar of Sedgeley*. The author was John Cornfeld Junior and he described the tithe as,

> "A certain tax, being a kind of buckseesh (sic) levied on every house-holder for the privilege of being allowed to live in the parish."

He describes how the vicar had seized goods from a defaulter and sold them, pocketing a profit over the tithe due. He had taken the bed from under one tithe defaulter, and billed Cornfeld for tax on land which, he claimed, carried no tithe. The entire volume seems to have been written in a white heat of passion:

"If the Vicar is determined to stick to his creed and stand or fall by it, let him take his place among the Herods, Pilates, Jeffries, Bonners and a host of others of the same creed who in every age and country have been the plagues of society; for he has done to me and others all that the law allowed him and none of these characters have done more. Some, however, may here urge that the Vicar has not put anyone to death for his religious opinions; and why has he not done so? Chiefly because the law won't allow him to do that."

At the time Cornfeld was hurling his abuse at the Vicar of Sedgeley, there was widespread dissent against the tithe all over England. Half a century earlier things had been different in that protest was more local, but hatred of the tithe by small farmers was just as deep as Cornfeld's.

The incumbent of Oddingley in 1806 was the Reverend Mr Parker, who seems to have pursued his tithes with the same enthusiasm as the Reverend Lewis and been just as cordially hated.

On Old Midsummer's Day, 24th June of that year, a shot was heard in the vicar's garden and a cry of, 'Murder!' Neighbours rushed to the spot in time to find their vicar dead, his clothes still smouldering from the closeness of the shot. The perpetrator was in the act of running away. One villager gave chase but the murderer turned and threatened him with a pistol, which changed the pursuer's mind. The gunman flung his pistol over a hedge and fled, but not before he had been recognised as Richard Hemming, a wheelright and carpenter from Droitwich.

Richard Hemming got clear away. Fifty guineas was offered for information leading to his capture and, as events proved, there may have been many who could have claimed that huge reward, but none did. No one seemed able to explain the murder, insofar as there was no known connection between Hemming and the Vicar of Oddingley.

Nearly a quarter of a century passed before the real nature of the incident was revealed. In the years following the end of the Reverend Parker a more benevolent incumbent let the local farmers enjoy more of their profits. One who took the wrong form of advantage of this relaxation was Farmer Clewes of Netherwood Farm. Certainly he no longer paid such a heavy tithe, but he frittered away his income at the public house until, by 1830, he was forced to sell his farm.

The porch of Oddingley's church.
The tower is under repair

'Murder will out' declares the proverb, and there do seem to be a lot of occasions when a concealed killing has come to light through some long coincidence. So it was in Oddingley. The fate of the Reverend Parker might have remained a mystery for ever, but for the fact that the new owner of Netherwood Farm started building improvements which disturbed the floor of a barn, where his builder found human bones.

There was no way to determine the age of buried bones but the authorities were put on the right track. A distinctive belt buckle amongst the remains was instantly recognised by the builder, Hemming's brother in law. Hemming's widow also identified the skeleton by its teeth.

The question now arose as to how a man who had long been thought to have fled to some distant part of Britain, if not abroad, had been lying dead under Clewes's barn. Clewes was arrested and a bizarre tale emerged. He admitted that he had been part of a conspiracy by five Oddingley farmers who, driven to desperation by the Reverend Parker's tithing, had decided to murder him. The originator of the plan had been 70 year old Captain Evans, a half pay officer of the 89th Foot, owner of Church Farm and a Droitwich magistrate.

Evans' plot was supposedly hatched in the snug of the God Speed the Plough inn at Tibberton, where the Captain met with Clewes, John Bennett, Joseph Taylor and George Banks. A picturesque legend has it that when the plot was agreed the conspirators toasted its success. They did so with their drinks in their left hands, leaving their sword hands free and marking the toast as one that meant ill to somebody. Hemming was just the paid hitman.

Once the deed had been committed in broad daylight and Hemming identified as the killer, he became a danger to his employers. They met him at Clewes's barn where he asked for help in fleeing to America. At some point tempers were raised and, according to Clewes, Joseph Taylor killed Hemming. It is alleged that Captain Evans told Taylor, 'Well done, boy! I will give thee another glass or two of brandy', an odd remark if the killing was really by accident. Far more likely that the plotters decided to rid themselves of a dangerous loose end.

Hemming was safe from hanging and so were two of his pay-masters who had gone to join him on some far eternal, or infernal, shore. But there were still three who could be tried, starting with Clewes.

To the astonishment of many, not least his own, Clewes was released. One account says this was because Taylor, the principal in the crime, was dead, so the accessories could not be made to plead. For the same reason no proceedings were brought against the other two survivors.

This reasoning depended on the assumption that the deceased Joseph Taylor was really the killer of Hemmings. The only evidence on the point would be that of the other conspirators, and the Crown probably assumed that they would give evidence to this effect which the Crown could not counter.

Even so, the conclusion that Clewes and the others could not be charged was legal nonsense. It was, and is, perfectly possible to convict people of conspiring 'with a person or persons unknown', let alone a known but dead co-conspirator. Cynics believe to this day that the wealth of the survivors swung the balance in their favour.

Having escaped the rope, Clewes took up innkeeping at the Fir Tree Inn in Dunhampstead.

Speed the Plough

The discovery that Mr Parker had died because of his tithe collecting habits was only seven years before the Reverend Mr Lewis took up the incumbency of Sedgeley. You might have thought that he would have heard of the case and moderated his relationships with his parishioners, but it seems not. The greedy Mr Parker must have been forgotten, though a small reminder of him can still be seen at Netherwood Farm where his initials and the date of his death are cut on a stone set into a wall. An even less obvious reminder can be found in the name of a pub. Once the details of the crime were exposed, the landlord of the God Speed the Plough Inn at Tibberton removed the word 'God' from his sign, and Speed the Plough it is today.

'Time will reveal the dreadful secret.'
(Hayton, Notts 1937)

You cannot, in theory, be tried twice for the same crime in
England. In practice, if you are tried and the Jury cannot agree
a verdict, you may be tried again. Again, if you are convicted
and appeal, the Court of Appeal may order a re-trial. In reality
the rule comes down to this, that if you have been *acquitted* of
a crime, you cannot be tried for it again.

Despite that long standing practice the eminent forensic
pathologist, Sir Bernard Spilsbury, referred to Frederick
Nodder as 'the only man who has in effect been tried twice
in this country for the same murder'.

Nodder was a strange and mysterious man. A motor mechanic
by trade, he was said to have served with the Army Service Corps
during the Great War. In 1934 he was living in Sheffield, lodging
with a couple called Grimes. Nodder called himself Hudson but the
Grimes's knew his real name. He was married but had abandoned
his wife and child and was dodging a bastardy warrant, which may
account for his alias. At that time he was believed to be in his
early 40s.

Late in the summer of 1935 he moved from Sheffield to
Newark where he lodged for a short time with Mrs Grimes's
sister, a Mrs Tinsley whose husband was a coal haulier. Nodder
had been described as 'squalid', 'sordid' and 'evil', but for some
reason the Tinsley children liked him and called him Uncle
Fred.

In June of 1936 Frederick Nodder moved to the village of Hayton,
near Retford, and rented a house called Peacehaven. He used his
own name and worked for a haulage firm until sacked for drink
and dishonesty.

Although Mrs Grimes from Sheffield visited him at Peacehaven
as often as once a week, he saw nothing of the Tinsleys after
he left their home until January 1937.

At 4.00 pm on 5th January 1937, Mona Lilian Tinsley aged 10 left
school and set out for her home. Around that time a neighbour of
the Tinsleys who knew Nodder saw him loitering by the school
gate. Half an hour later a boy who attended the same school and
also knew Nodder saw him with Mona at Newark bus station.

After those two clear sightings by friends, all that remains of Mona's story is in the recollection of strangers. A bus conductor remembered seeing her that afternoon with Nodder on the bus from Retford to Newark. Two men remembered seeing Nodder and the little girl that evening in Retford. A maid who worked two doors from Peacehaven saw a little girl at Nodder's back door next morning. That was the last time she was seen alive.

Questioned by the Police on 6th January, Nodder said that he had not seen Mona Tinsley for fifteen months. Two days later he changed his mind - he had met Mona by chance in Newark as she made her way home from school on 5th January. His story went on; Mrs Grimes had a baby boy about 9 months old which she was bringing to Peacehaven the next day on one of her weekly visits. Mona was anxious to see the baby, so kindly Uncle Fred took her the twenty miles from Newark to Retford to stay overnight and see the baby, without telling her parents. The following morning he had received a note from Mrs Grimes cancelling her visit that week, so he thought it best to send Mona on to her aunt's home in Sheffield, again without telling her parents.

The bastardy warrant was still out for him in Sheffield, so Nodder did not want to be seen there. He took Mona as far as Worksop where he left her on a bus to Sheffield with 2 shillings (10p) and instructions for finding Mrs Grimes' home. At least, he thought it was a Sheffield bus, but didn't seem certain. Going back to Retford he had a few drinks before going home, where he was met by the Police.

The Grimes' said that they knew nothing of this, but they also said that they did not know where Nodder lived, despite Mrs Grimes' weekly visits. These, it seems, had something to do with some obscure (and probably illegal) transaction involving lorries. However, the strange relationships between Nodder, who Spilsbury describes as 'a disgusting creature of filthy habits', and the Grimes and Tinsley families were never properly unravelled.

Peacehaven was almost taken apart, brick by brick, and its garden thoroughly dug over by the Police, but they found no sign of little Mona. A massive search began, though few doubted that Nodder had abducted and murdered the child. In the meantime, and in the belief that Mona's body would soon be found, Nodder was charged on 10th January 1937 with abduction. On the following day

NEWARK BOROUGH POLICE

Telephone No. 26

CHIEF CONSTABLE'S OFFICE,
TOWN HALL,
NEWARK-ON-TRENT.
11th JANUARY, 1937

MISSING FROM HER HOME

at 11, Thoresby Avenue, Newark-on-Trent, since Tuesday, 5th January, 1937, MONA LILIAN TINSLEY. age 10 years (rather short for age), dark hair, (bobbed with fringe), rosy cheeks, four prominent teeth at front.   Dress, when last seen, light blue woollen jumper suit, brown double breasted tweed coat (frayed at bottom of sleeves), black Wellington boots, no hat, white half hose, dark blue knickers, white liberty bodice, white cotton underskirt, woollen combinations. was carrying a brown or grey handbag which contained a birthday card with figure " 10 " thereon. It has been established that this girl was seen at Hayton Smeath, near Retford, Notts. at about mid-day on Wednesday, 6th January, 1937, since when all trace of her has been lost. It has been suggested that she travelled to Sheffield on a bus leaving Retford at 6.45 p.m.

Any person who has seen this girl, or the clothing described above, since Wednesday mid-day is asked to get in touch with the nearest police officer immediately.

HARRY   BARNES,
CHIEF CONSTABLE.

J. STENNETT, PRINTER, NEWARK.

Newark Police issued a handbill with the child's photograph and a detailed description of her clothing when she disappeared.

Police officers and volunteers continued searching for the child through weeks of a vile, wet winter. Mona's parents called on a medium, Estelle Roberts, who said that the child had been murdered and her body dumped in a river, but she could not tell them which one.

This area is low lying and veined with waterways. Apart from the rivers Ryton and Idle, there is the Chesterfield Canal and a multitude of little streams, and many of them were dragged. Woods and copses covered the area and also had to be searched. Day in and day out, rain slashed the area, ditches overflowed, rivers swelled, and the peaceful Idle became a foaming flood half a mile wide.

It is no surprise that Mona was not found, and so no charge of murder was brought against Nodder. Instead, on 9th March 1937, he appeared before Mr Justice Swift at the Victoria Law Courts, Birmingham, for trial on abduction charges.

He was defended by Maurice Healy KC and prosecuted by Norman Birkett KC, still admired as one of the greatest cross examiners. But Birkett was to be robbed of any opportunity to demonstrate his skills, for Nodder did not give evidence. His counsel, says one report, was treated by the Judge with 'brusqueness and acerbity'.

In his summing up Mr Justice Swift went beyond brusqueness and acerbity and trod far into the realm of illegality in his desire to see Nodder convicted. He told the Jury:

> "Nobody knows what has become of that little girl....
> Whatever happened to her, how she fared, who looked
> after her, where she slept, there is one person in this
> court who knows, and he is silent, he is silent. He
> says nothing to you at all... he sits there and never
> tells you a word."

An important measure of a society's civilisation is the protection it gives to people suspected of crime. Mere revenge is easy, the most barbarous societies can track down suspects to be tortured or killed. For centuries, until it was abolished recently so as to provide greater opportunities to confuse and entrap a suspect, English law afforded an accused person the protection of the so called 'right to silence'. Simply put, this meant that failure to answer questions under interrogation or failure to give evidence before a court could not, must not, be taken as evidence of guilt. Nor must it be suggested to a Jury that it might be.

Mr Justice Swift had not only torn that protection away from Nodder, he had virtually given evidence for the Prosecution by his assertion that 'there is one person in this court who knows', a statement that utterly subverted Nodder's defence. However repulsive he was, however wicked the crime with which he was charged, however much worse the crime with which he had not been charged, Nodder was entitled to better treatment than he received at Swift's hands.

The Jury, whether through the Judge's direction or more probably through the weakness of the defence, had no difficulty in convicting Nodder. In sentencing him Mr Justice Swift again revealed his inability to deal only with the matters before the court. Sentencing Nodder to seven years in prison he said:

"What you did with that little girl, what became of her, only you know. It may be that time will reveal the dreadful secret which you carry in your breast."

Nodder appealed in the light of the Judge's behaviour and should have won a retrial, but his application was dismissed.

Three months passed and the rain slackened, the rivers slowed and fell. On Sunday 6th June a party rowing down the Idle from Bawtry saw Mona Tinsley's floating body, about 10 winding miles from the point where the river passes within a mile of Hayton.

Mr Tinsley identified his daughter's remains and next day Dr J M Webster, the Birmingham pathologist, carried out an examination. While he did so, Mona's coat and one of her rubber boots were dredged up near where the body was found.

Sir Bernard Spilsbury travelled from London and joined in the scientific examinations. Time and great care were taken. Nodder had escaped being charged with murder once, and the Police were anxious that the evidence would convict him when they did charge him. By 29th July all was ready and Nodder was charged with Mona's murder.

His second trial began at Nottingham Assizes in November 1937. Once again, Norman Birkett led the Prosecution and Maurice Healy the Defence. Most of the evidence was identical to the Birmingham trial, apart from that of the scientists.

Dr Webster described his first sight of the remains and the finding of a horizontal mark running around the neck of the body. He said that adipocere (a waxy substance that derives from chemical changes after death) had formed, and that since this change took place slowly, he believed he could estimate that the body had been in the water five or six months.

Once the body was cleaned he had found that the horizontal mark did not meet at the back of the neck. It was, he thought, the mark of a thin ligature being tied about the neck before death. The tongue bore teeth marks, and he believed that pressure of the cord or string had forced the tongue up, causing it to be bitten. Mona had been healthy and he was satisfied that she had not died naturally or from drowning, but by strangulation.

At his first trial Nodder had achieved nothing by saying nothing. His stance had been that he could not know what had happened to Mona after he put her on the Sheffield bus. Now he took up a different defence. Mr Healy cross examined Dr Webster on the basis that Mona might accidentally have caught her clothing in a branch and so strangled. Webster deemed it unlikely and pointed out that in such a case the mark would have been oblique, not horizontal.

Spilsbury supported Webster's view that death was by strangulation, probably from behind, so that the ligature had not been in contact with the back of the neck. The tongue markings, he said, would disappear so rapidly in a living person that they must have been made immediately before death. He disposed of the 'accident' theory by pointing out that Mona's clothing had no narrow upper edge that could have caused the mark, and agreeing with Webster that the mark of a suspension would have been oblique.

The Defence called one witness, Frederick Nodder. In the predecessor to this book, *Midland Murders & Mysteries,* I described Norman Birkett's cross examination of Alfred Rouse. Nodder was nowhere near so tough. All he could do was cling to his story that he had put Mona on what he thought was the bus to

Sheffield and that, if she was murdered, it must have happened near Worksop where the River Ryton flows into the Idle south of Bawtry.

The evidence all in, the Crown could present a damning series of facts backed by eminent expert opinion. The Defence had only Nodder's wholly unsatisfactory story and the suggestion that Mona had been killed after Nodder left her. Mr Justice Macnaghten pointed out to the Jury that no expert evidence had been called by the Defence, which strongly suggested that Webster and Spilsbury were right in saying that Mona was murdered. He asked them to consider whether the facts proved before them were consistent with any explanation other than murder by Nodder.

The Jury retired and then something very unusual happened. They were recalled to the Court to hear additional evidence. Now a Jury are judges of the facts in a case and can, as they sometimes do, ask for further evidence on a point. When they do the Judge will try to see that it is made available. However, it is almost unheard of for evidence for the Crown or Defence to be called after a Judge has given the case to the Jury.

That is what happened at Nottingham. The Defence asked to call back the witness who had found Mona's body on 6th June. Presumably because it was a Defence application in a capital murder case, the Judge allowed the evidence.

The witness now said that, a week or two before 6th June he and his sons had been boating on the Ryton, close to the junction with the Idle. They had seen a large sack awash on a mudbank which was giving off an offensive stench. Obviously the calling of this evidence was to support Nodder's contention that Mona had been killed in or near Worksop and flung into the Ryton. The Crown recalled Dr Webster, who reminded the Jury that Mona's body had not begun to decompose before it was put into the water. The production of adipocere in a corpse produces only a faint, musty smell, not the reek of putrefaction.

The Jury retired again but returned in thirty minutes with a guilty verdict. Sentenced to death Nodder, appealed again and was again refused. On 30th December 1937 he was hanged at Lincoln Prison.

'With dog and gun and snare.'
(Ryton on Dunsmore, Warks 1858)

No full account of this murder has ever been published, and it would never have come to light but for the work of Gary Moore who lives in Nuneaton.

Researching his family history he discovered that by and large, they seemed to have lead fairly ordinary and undramatic lives. However, Gary had some difficulty in tracing his great great grandfather. When eventually Joseph Owen's death certificate was traced the cause of death was recorded as, 'Murdered by persons unknown'.

Gary began a trawl through newspaper archives and legal records and uncovered a rambling but complete account of a Coroner's Inquest held at Ryton on Dunsmore in 1858. There was a mass of confusing testimony from a large number of witnesses, but when Gary reduced it to order he discovered an unsolved murder mystery.

After reading *Midland Murders & Mysteries* he sent his manuscript to my publisher, John Roberts. Through no fault of Gary's it was an awkward sized package, too short to make a book on its own and too long to fit into a collection. I therefore spent many hours pruning and summarising, abbreviating and removing duplications to arrive at what follows. Many thanks Gary, for a fascinating story.

*

William Shakespeare fled from Warwickshire to avoid prosecution for poaching, so they say. Nearly three hundred years later, another Warwickshire man's fate at the hands of the law was recorded in song:

> Come all you wild and wicked lads
> That ramble free from care,
> That walk at night in the bright moonlight
> With dog and gun and snare,
> I'll tell you of our sufferings,
> That you may understand,
> The hardships we do undergo
> Upon Van Diemen's Land.

Me and three more companions went
To Squire Daniels' park.
To take some game was our intent,
As the night came falling dark;
But we were quickly taken there,
By keepers with all speed,
And carried straight to Warwick Gaol,
Which made our hearts to bleed.

'Twas at the March Assizes,
Our trial we did bear.
Like Job we stood in patience,
Our sentence for to hear,
And being wellknown offenders,
Our case it did go hard,
Our sentence was full fourteen years
And we were sent on board.

Like Shakespeare, the subject of this song was an educated man.
Later in the song we learn that Henry Abbott became a book
keeper in Van Diemen's Land, or Tasmania, but education had
not helped him at his trial. He had transgressed against
England's near sacred law of property.

We tend to think of poachers as quaint rural characters, practit-
ioners of a dying craft, like thatchers, hedgers and wattle makers.
Perhaps so, but they were once regarded by the landed gentry,
and the law, as serious villains bent on looting other people's
property.

For centuries until the law was liberalised, war was waged in
the fields and woods of England. Sentences for poaching included
prison, hanging and transportation for life to Van Dieman's Land
(now Tasmania), and their severity guaranteed that poachers would
avoid arrest by any means, including killing. Gamekeepers, watch-
men and poachers were the casualties, suffering beatings, maimings
and often death by mantrap, cudgel, knife or shotgun. Another
victim of that long war met his death at Ryton on Dunsmore,
Warwickshire early in the summer of 1858.

Sunday 9th May was cold and wet. At 6.10 am the dreary morning
was disturbed by a boy banging on the door of Ryton Lodge Farm
and shouting about finding a body.

10th May - First Hearing

The Coroner's Inquest sat next day at the Bull & Butcher public house, Ryton on Dunsmore, and the jury viewed the body of Joseph Owen, farm labourer. His face was blackened, his whiskers slightly singed and a gunshot wound ran through his neck from left to right. It was larger on the right side than the left, showing that the gun had been fired close to Joseph's left ear. Death must have been immediate.

Joseph Owen's ancestors had worked the canals around Birmingham and Coventry since they opened in the late 18th century, but he had tried to make more of his life. He had set out on a journey around the Coventry area where he met, and in October 1851 married, Mary Lissaman, daughter of a Wolston carpenter. He worked as an agricultural labourer around Wolston, and between 1851 and 1857 the couple had three sons.

In December 1857 Joseph found a job working for Thomas Boddington, a farmer at Ryton on Dunsmore. After five months Joseph had shown that he was a hard working man. Boddington was having problems with poachers and told Joseph to keep a lookout, late at night and early in the morning. This extra work began in the first week of May 1858. Locals referred to him as the "Looker Outer".

Mr Newbold, the farmer at Ryton Lodge, was the first witness. He told the Inquest how he was aroused by the boy and had gone to the window in his nightshirt. Then a man called Morley ran into the farmyard, also shouting about a body. Morley said the man had been shot.

Mr Newbold did not know Morley and cautiously asked if he had a gun. Morley said that he didn't, unbuttoning his jacket and holding it open. Satisfied, Newbold dressed and accompanied Morley and the boy. On their way they passed two other people, later named as Glenn and Calcott, who seemed very happy and pleased with themselves. Newbold asked if they had been poaching, adding that they need not deny it as he had seen their bag with blood on it.

1851. Marriage solemnized at the Parish Church in the Parish of Ashchurch Leamington in the County of Warwick

No.	When Married	Name and Surname	Age	Condition	Rank or Profession	Residence at the Time of Marriage	Father's Name and Surname	Rank or Profession of Father
80	October 13 1851	Joseph Owen	23	Bachelor	Laborer	St John Street	Samuel Owen	Laborer
		Mary Liverman	23	Spinster		St John Street	Charles Liverman	Carpenter

Married in the Parish Church according to the Rites and Ceremonies of the Established Church, by _____ or after Banns _____ by me, William Doolittle

This Marriage was solemnized between us, Joseph Owen / Mary Liverman her X mark

in the Presence of us, William Doolittle / Elizabeth Smith her X mark

---

Registration District Rugby

1858. Death in the Sub-district of Dunchurch in the County of Warwick

	No.	When and where died	Name and surname	Sex	Age	Occupation	Cause of death	Signature, description, and residence of informant	When registered	Signature of registrar
Columns:—	1	2	3	4	5	6	7	8	9
	209	Ninth May 1858 Ryton-on-Dunsmore	Joseph Owen	Male	32 Years	Servant in Husbandry	Wilfully Murdered by Some Person or Persons Unknown	Wm Savage Poole Coroner Kenilworth	Twenty Third June 1858	Thomas White Registrar

*Copies of the marriage and death certificates of Joseph Owen.
Joseph could just about sign his name but Mary could not.
Take good note of the name of the first witness.*

Edward Parker was a boy who helped with Mr Newbold's sheep. His evidence was that he had been on his way to work at about 6.00 am when he saw a body in the road some distance ahead. Three men were moving towards him, about 200 yards off when he saw them going towards Coventry. When they reached the body they called to him, 'There's a man dead, come and look'. They frightened him and he ran to get Mr Newbold.

Joseph's body lay on the road about two fields from Ryton. He was within a yard of the grass verge with his feet pointing towards Ryton Lodge. His right hand clutched a walking stick, which extended across the road, his left was in his jacket pocket and his head lay in a pool of blood. His features were fixed. There did not seem to have been a struggle. Although it was raining, Newbold searched the area and found marks near some bushes, which suggested that someone had lain in wait for quite some time.

Chief Constable Isaac arrived swiftly with his deputy, Mr Small-bone. They searched the area, conducted an enquiry and then arrested William Ringrose and Thomas Kimberley on suspicion of murder. What led the Police to these two has never been revealed. Maybe they were 'wellknown offenders' or perhaps were simply known to have been poaching on the previous night.

These hasty arrests wasted an enormous amount of time at the inquest and may have confused events so as to protect the real killer. The evidence showed that the local woods and fields were swarming with poachers that night.

Mrs Jane Allen gave her testimony. She lived near where the body was found. She had heard someone talking loudly, then the report of a gun followed by silence at about 3.45 am on the Sunday.

Owen's employer, Thomas Boddington, was examined next. He held the shooting rights of the Manor from the owner, Mr Featherstone Dilke. Joseph Owen worked for him and kept a lookout for poachers early in the morning and late at night. He was not aware of Joseph having crossed words with anyone.

The Coroner then adjourned the inquest to 18th May for a post mortem, the hearing to be at the Blacksmith's Arms in Ryton, because the room at the Bull & Butcher was not large enough for the crowd. A reward of £100 was offered for discovery of the murderer.

18th May - Second Hearing

When the inquest reopened the first witness was Mr Blanshard, surgeon of Wolston. He had found no marks of violence except the gunshot wound to the neck, beginning a little below the left ear and passing obliquely downward and forward to the opposite side. The left opening was round and about an inch in diameter, but the right side wound was larger and ragged. The whiskers on the left were singed. The right wound was about an inch lower and an inch further forward than the left. He found in the wound twenty pieces of lead shot, which he produced; some were larger than others, and they were all flattened and bruised.

Mr Blanshard had no doubt that the gunshot wound was the cause of death, and he presumed that Joseph must have fallen instantly because there was no blood on his jacket. It was clear from the wound that the man was shot on the left side. The whiskers were singed, suggesting that the gun had been fired about a foot from Joseph's ear, and must have inclined downwards. If the man had shot himself the wound would have run upwards. He agreed that the wound might have been caused by a pistol.

The Inquest seemed to have clear enough evidence as to when, where and how Joseph Owen was killed, and there seemed to be no conflicts or difficulties about it. Confusion set in with the evidence of the many midnight wanderers who seem to have lurked behind every hedge that night. The map may help a little.

The next witness was William Glenn who worked at Coventry Waterworks. Soon after 9.00 pm on Saturday 8th May he left Coventry with Calcott and Morley. [The three mentioned by the farmer.] They were out all night, separating shortly after 3.00 am.

He walked about for some time, heard the Nunnery clock (at Princethorpe Priory) strike 5.00 am and rejoined his companions as arranged, on the Coventry side of Princethorpe near Bull & Butcher Wood. They went through the wood and were getting near the top, not far from Stretton, when they heard the report of a gun and saw some tame pigeons fly. They saw somebody run, but could not tell if it was a man or a boy. About three quarters of a mile beyond the body Glenn saw two men dressed in dark clothes heading for Coventry.

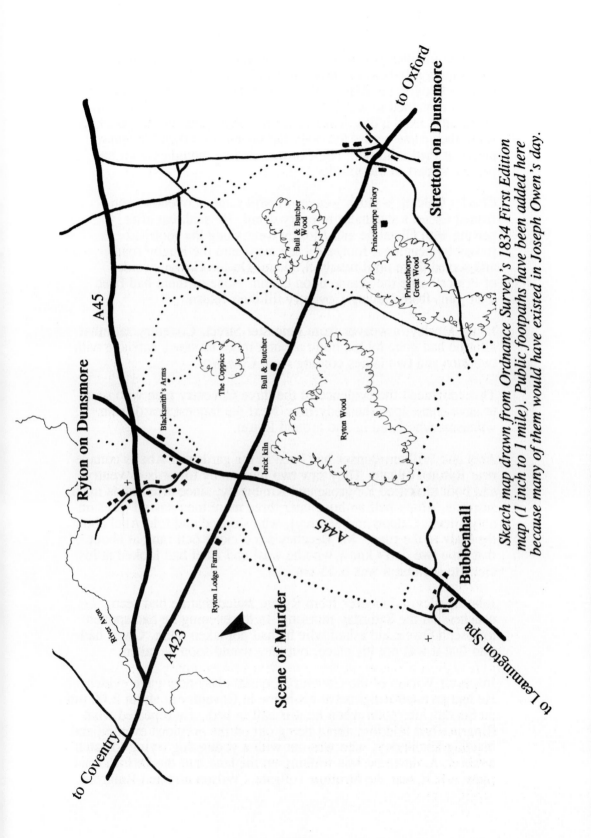

to Oxford

Stretton on Dunsmore

to Coventry

Ryton on Dunsmore

A45

A423

RIVER AVON

Blacksmith's Arms

The Coppice

Bull & Butcher

brick kiln

Ryton Wood

Bull & Butcher Wood

Princethorpe Priory

Princethorpe Great Wood

Ryton Lodge Farm

Scene of Murder

A45

Bubbenhall

to Leamington Spa

Sketch map drawn from Ordnance Survey's 1834 First Edition map (1 inch to 1 mile). Public footpaths have been added here because many of them would have existed in Joseph Owen's day.

At a few minutes past 6.00 am, a few yards beyond the four ways road junction [where the modern A455 crosses the A423] Glenn saw Owen's body in the road. Glenn and Calcott gave the alarm, while Morley remained to watch the body. Calcott carried a bag with blood on it from a dead hare. They had their guns in their pockets when they came across the body but Glenn had taken his gun to pieces at Princethorpe. The Coroner said he thought Glenn had played no part in the murder.

Charles Calcott, a plush weaver of Mill Lane, Coventry, con-firmed Glenn's statement in every detail. He said that after parting with Glenn he and Morley went along the footroad [possibly meaning a footpath - see map] into the Rugby road, and stayed there until nearly 5.00 am. On the Coventry side of Princethorpe they came upon Glenn. None of them had fired their guns from leaving Coventry till their return.

James Morley, a weaver from Leicester Street, Coventry said that after he had gone by the body about a mile, he saw a carriage with two men and two ladies coming from Coventry.

This concluded the evidence of the three Coventry men who seem to have come upon the body first. Next the Inquest heard from witnesses who lived in and around Ryton.

Abel and William Bonsor had been in the garden of Abel's cottage near Ryton Tollgate. They saw two men go by towards Coventry and both identified Ringrose and Kimberley, since arrested as main suspects. About half an hour later three more men passed [presum-ably Glenn, Calcott and Morley], who stopped and told Abel about the body in the road. Mr Beechey's 6 o'clock bell rang at about that time [we don't know who he was] and Abel had looked at his clock to see that it was 6.15 am.

John Beasley, a labourer from Ryton, stated that he had seen poachers on the Saturday morning. In the evening he had spoken to Joseph Owen and asked why he had not taken them. Owen had said that it was not his place, but they would soon be taken.

Inspector Wilson of the Coventry Constabulary now gave evidence. He had arrested Ringrose at his home in Coventry at about 2.00 pm on Sunday afternoon when he was still in bed. He repeated what Ringrose had told him about being out on the previous evening and meeting Kimberley, who was out with a young dog trying to catch a rabbit. At dawn he was walking up the lane into the Oxford road [now A423] near the Stretton Tollgate. Wilson arrested Ringrose and searched his house, finding a loaded gun hanging over the fireplace but covered with dust, and a velveteen shooting coat which he produced. Ringrose said he had worn it on the night in question. In the right hand pocket was a powder flask, and in the other pocket, gate nets.

Mr Smallbone, Deputy Chief Constable and Superintendent of Police at Rugby, said that he had heard of the crime on the Sunday and gone straight to Kimberley's house in Coventry to arrest him on suspicion. Kimberley said that he had been out all night with Ringrose, and that Inspector Wilson had already been to his home and questioned him. Most of what Kimberley said supported Ringrose's statement.

Smallbone found a loaded gun at Kimberley's house and thought it had been fired in the last forty eight hours, but he was not certain. There were two other guns in the house, both rusty and dusty. The Superintendent found no powder and shot and no signs of blood on Kimberley's clothes. Kimberley was taken to the lock up.

Smallbone and James Kenlon, a turnkey at Coventry Jail, both gave evidence of remarks by Ringrose made to them and to a fellow prisoner. He had declared his innocence and given seemingly contradictory accounts of seeing or not seeing a gun fired and a man fall.

26th May - Third Hearing

The Coroner's Inquest continued on 26th May, by which time John Franklin, a carrier from Ryton had been arrested.

Michael Brannon, John O'Neill and John Bryan, Irish labourers, told how they had left Coventry at about 4.30 am on the Sunday making for Leamington Hastings. At the turn of the Oxford road they saw two men with dogs, one man carrying a bundle, but they could not identify them. They went on past a farmhouse and came upon the body of a dead man. A farmer present asked if they had seen anyone on the road, and Brannon described the two men as best he could.

William Smith, labourer, from Bubbenhall was examined next He said that he knew the prisoner, John Franklin, and was in Franklin's company on the morning of the murder and the previous night. They first met in the Blacksmith's Arms at

Ryton about midnight, then went to Franklin's cottage. They took three pints of beer which Franklin, his wife and himself drank with their supper. They talked for two or two and a half hours, than at about 2.30 am he and Franklin left to go to Smith's own home. They went in the direction of Bubbenhall. Franklin had said, 'I shall try to kill a rabbit'. Smith asked, 'Have you a ferret?' Franklin said, 'No'.

As they got to Bagshaw's Barn near the Oxford road, Franklin pulled out a gun. They stayed together as far as Collins' Gutter, where they parted at about 3.15 am. Smith said he went home and arrived about 3.45. He could not say where Franklin acquired the gun. He did not know Franklin had a gun on him until he had pulled it out by Bagshaw's Barn.

Franklin had been wearing a dark coat and his gun was a short one. Smith had not seen it before that morning. He had last seen Franklin with a gun two or three years earlier at a pigeon shoot. Franklin did not fire the gun whilst Smith was in his company, as far as he was aware. [A strange thing to say.] He could not remember if Franklin's wife had asked him not to go out that morning.

Smith said that he next saw Franklin on Sunday night at 7.30 at Franklin's cottage. Franklin said that the Police had asked him where he had been and what time he had arrived home. Apart from that, little else was said about the incident. Smith never asked Franklin what time he had got home, and he never enquired about the gun. Smith was well acquainted with Joseph Owen and had spoken to him frequently. Franklin had not told Smith that he had heard that Owen intended to catch him poaching, and that he, Franklin, would "serve him out".

Smith admitted that on the morning of the murder he had fired a gun, but said that he had not taken it out with him and Franklin earlier. He had not seen Franklin's gun since the morning of the murder. While they were at Franklin's cottage [he seems to have meant before their nocturnal outing] the butcher had called and left two half shoulders of mutton.

William Kenning was a labourer from Bubbenhall living next door but one to William Smith. He confirmed that Smith had arrived home at 3.45 am and had rapped Kenning's window as he went by.

Samuel Smith, a labourer, was examined next. His cottage was only a few yards away from Franklin's. He had seen Franklin near his home at about 5.30 am when he was on the way to his gardens on the Oxford road. Franklin had been wearing the same waistcoat that he always wore and had not spoken to him. He said that Franklin and Joseph Owen were good friends.

Joseph Hobday was Franklin's brother in law. He gave evidence that Franklin had been to his house and borrowed a short barrelled gun about three feet long from Mrs Hobday. He said that he kept his powder in a flask and his shot in a leather pouch, and he would recognise both the flask and pouch if he saw them. He did not know what had happened to the gun, the flask or the pouch. They were never returned.

The next witness was Chief Constable Isaac. He said that acting on 'information received', he and Superintendent Smallbone went on 19th May to a garden near a brick yard on the Oxford road where John Franklin was hoeing. Isaac cautioned him, then asked where he had been on the evening before and on the morning of the murder.

Franklin said that he had been out searching for his escaped horses [he was a carrier] along the Oxford road. He had got up about 7.00 am having gone to bed at 2.30. On the eve of the murder he had been drinking at the Blacksmith's Arms with Eli Stretton and William Smith until about midnight. Stretton went back to his house and Smith went with Franklin. He remembered the butcher coming, having supper and Smith leaving at about 2.30.

Franklin denied having had a gun for two months. He said that Smith had been to his house on the Sunday evening wanting to know what time he had left, because he could not remember. The two policemen arrested Franklin and his house was searched, but they found no gun, powder or shot.

Thomas Kimberley was one of the suspects who had been arrested and he was examined next. He lived at Herbert's Row in Coventry. On the night before the murder he had left Coventry at about 8.30 pm and was walking in the direction of Ryton when he met Ringrose at the Wall Close at the back of the Charter House. Ringrose had with him a dog and a gate net, as did Kimberley. They carried on towards Ryton. Neither he nor Ringrose had firearms of any description with them. At dawn they sheltered under a hawthorn bush beyond Mr Newbold's farm house. There they heard the report of a gun and thought that it came from the direction of the crossroads.

They saw something in the road, but couldn't tell whether it was a horse or a man. They returned to Coventry and parted company at the Wall Close as the church clock struck 7.00 am.

The Coroner said that neither he nor the Jury thought that Kimberley was the guilty party, Kimberley replying fervently, 'Thank God, I am innocent'.

William Ringrose, the second prisoner, confirmed Kimberley's testimony. He said that he had not been so far under the hedge as Kimberley, so saw the flash of a gun and the smoke, and afterwards heard the report. Before the gun was fired he saw a man on the left side of the road who seemed to have come over the fields. He was advancing in their direction. The smoke hung over the road for five minutes, and when it had cleared the man had disappeared.

Mrs Hobday of Ryton gave her evidence. She told the Inquest that she was John Franklin's sister. About two months ago her brother had asked if he could borrow her husband's gun. He had not taken any powder or shot. They did not have powder or shot anymore, but they had at that time and it was kept in the table drawer. Franklin wanted the powder and shot but Mrs Hobday would not let him have any because her husband would not allow it.

Asked what had become of the powder and shot, she replied, 'I don't know, it may be at home, I dare say it could be found'. The Coroner asked, 'Could you show it to a Police Officer, if he went with you?'. Mrs Hobday replied, 'No, I don't think I could'.

'Now look at me, in the face', said the Coroner, 'and tell me whether you knew that your brother had taken away both powder and shot'. With great reluctance Mrs Hobday gave in. 'He took away one charge of powder, and one or two charges of shot'. The Coroner asked, 'Could you find the flask and shot bag?', Mrs Hobday replied, 'I don't know'. The Coroner said, 'Well, you must try to find them, and give them to the Police Constable. It would be best for all parties if you tell the truth'.

The Inquest was adjourned again, to 1st June. Ringrose and Kimberley were both discharged. Their testimony and the evidence about them had done nothing to identify the killer of Joseph Owen and precious little to clarify events.

1st June - Fourth Hearing

At the next hearing the first witness was William Smith, who said that on the morning of the murder Franklin had worn a dark velveteen shooting jacket, but he could not say which of two produced was Franklin's.

Superintendent Smallbone [also Deputy Chief Constable] was examined and said that he had found no bloodmarks on either of the jackets. He had searched Franklin's premises but could not find the gun. He had gone with Mrs Hobday to their cottage, and on the way, Mrs Hobday had apparently decided to tell him everything. She said he need not go any further, as he would find no powder or shot. Her husband had removed them to, 'hide his blame'. Even so, Smallbone searched the premises carefully and found nothing.

Mrs Mary Owen, widow of Joseph Owen, said that as far as she could guess, Joseph had left home between 3.00 and 4.00 o'clock on the morning that he was murdered. He was not armed. She knew of no one with a grudge against him, and to the best of her belief he had not been on bad terms with John Franklin.

Mr George Mann, Governor of Coventry Jail, gave evidence that Franklin had written to his wife, Ann, on 28th May. It read:

My Dear Ann,

I have asked leave to write a few lines to you, hoping to find you well, as it leaves me at this present time, thank God for it. Respecting the gun you know you took from me six or seven weeks before this happened, what you done with it I don't know, but I hope you will give it up. The powder flask and shot bag, there is no shot, ask Joseph Hobday to bring his powder flask and shot bag. They need not be afraid of showing them; it has not been my wish, they have been kept back. So I hope you will have ready for Tuesday (sic), and be sure and meet me that morning.

My love to you, and for the children.

John Franklin.

Mrs Ann Franklin, wife of the prisoner, gave evidence.

"I found a gun in the stable about seven weeks ago, and
I concealed it from my husband, because I had heard that
Mr Boddington had said we should be turned out of the
cottage we occupied, if my husband was seen out with a
gun. About a fortnight ago, I gave the gun to Smith. He
promised me that my husband should never have it again,
and I said that he might keep it then. Smith was at our
cottage on the night before the murder; he had supper
with us and left at about half past two. I then went up
to bed, and I believe my husband followed, but I cannot
say for certain, as I fell asleep almost straight away.
I woke up at a quarter to six, my husband was dressing,
I cannot swear that he had been to bed. When he was
completely dressed, he was wearing his usual waistcoat,
the one he is wearing today. I heard nothing said at
supper about getting a rabbit, but Smith asked my
husband if he had a gun, he replied 'No'. I heard
nothing further said about the matter, I believed my
husband to be in bed that night, as he had told me so.
I was upstairs when Smith left, I only heard him leave.
When I heard that my husband had a gun, I hid it in a
chest upstairs, and kept it there till I gave it to
Smith".

Mrs Franklin was closely pressed by the Coroner but insisted that
she had given the gun to William Smith. He was at once recalled
to the witness stand and brought further confusion into the case:

Coroner: "You told me when you reached home on the
morning of the murder, that you fired a gun. Was that
the gun given to you by Mrs Franklin?"

Smith: "Yes, it is on the rack at home".

Coroner Poole ordered the weapon's immediate production.

Smith: "I did not mean to say that was the gun Mrs
Franklin gave me, she did not give me any gun at all".

Coroner: "But you said just now that she did!"

Smith: "No, I did not; I could not have understood the
question".

Mrs Franklin now intervened in the confusion:

> Mrs Franklin: "Can you look me in the face and say I did not give you a gun?"

> Smith: "Yes I can".

Neither party would back down and Smith was ordered from the room. The Coroner repeated his order for production of the gun and Mrs Franklin concluded her evidence by saying, 'I told Hobday that if he did not get his gun again, I would pay him for it'.

Robert Watts, a labourer of Ryton, gave evidence. He had seen Franklin about fifty yards from his cottage at 6.40 on the morning of the murder. Watts had not then heard about the murder. Franklin said, 'What the bloody hell is up this morning? Something about a shooting'. Watts said he didn't know what it was, and Franklin said, 'Somebody had been shooting a man'. John Bull had been into Kemp's and told him about it.

Franklin said he should go and see about it. He went on a short way but turned back two or three times. He looked very frightened and seemed as if he had something to say. He afterwards went to look at the body. Franklin was wearing a clean pair of boots but the bottoms of his trousers were wet. He had helped lift the body onto a cart.

Mrs Kemp was examined and said that on the morning of the murder she had told Franklin about it, and he had said he would go and see the body. She had noticed nothing particular in his manner, and he did not seem as if he had already heard of the murder.

William Smith's gun was brought in and he identified it as his property, saying he bought it from a Mr Thomas Bell. Mrs Franklin was recalled and said she could not say whether this was the gun given to Smith, but she thought not.

Thomas Bell was called. He said that the gun produced was his property and he had lent it to Franklin. It was Russian, from the Crimean War, and he had won it in a raffle.

Mrs Franklin was recalled, and insisted that she had given the Hobday's gun to Smith.

Smith was recalled and, after being pressed by the Foreman of the Jury, admitted that some months ago he called at Mrs Franklin's house and she had given him a gun to take care of. He promised that he would not let her husband see it and he took the gun to John Perkins, to whom he understood it belonged. He thought that this was more than 12 months before.

John Perkins, shoemaker, explained that he had lent a gun to Franklin about 12 months ago. Franklin's wife had said, 'She would make away with it, if he did not fetch it', he therefore went and got the gun from Mrs Franklin.

[So it seems three guns passed through Franklin's hands, those of Bell, Perkins and Hobday. Perkins recovered his some 12 months before the murder, but Smith may have held both Bell's and Hobday's.]

The Coroner then announced that the prisoner, Franklin, was willing to be examined, but there was a difficulty because the prisoner was in the custody of the Magistrates. In other words he was an accused person and as the law stood, the Coroner could not examine him. However, if Franklin wanted to make a written statement he might do so and the Coroner would use it or not, at his discretion. If it was not used it would be treated as confidential.

Mr Hobday was called to the stand again but only to deny that he knew what had become of the gun his wife had lent Franklin. Mrs Hobday was also recalled, and having been cautioned by the Coroner, said that though her brother, Franklin, borrowed the gun and took away a charge or two of powder and a charge of shot, she was quite sure he did not take away either the powder flask or shot bag. She could not tell what had become of them. The proceedings were adjourned to Wednesday 9th June.

'We understand', said the press, 'that the Chief Constable of the County is in possession of information which will throw great light on this hitherto, mysterious affair'. Events proved them wrong.

Fifth Hearing

The fifth hearing started with a reading of the statements already taken, which must have taken no little time. After Mrs Franklin's statement was read she was examined by her husband's solicitor.

Originally she had said that William Smith left her house at 2.30 am; she now said, 'It was nearer 4'. Before he left Smith remarked that he had a pistol in his pocket, although she had not seen it. Smith went to their house on Sunday night and told her to say that he had left at 2.30. He also told Franklin to deny that he went out with him or that he had seen him after he went away. Mrs Franklin said that she had slept from 2.30 until 5.45 in the morning, and she only knew that Smith had left at 4.00 because of what he had said on Sunday evening. Present at this conversation were Mr and Mrs Smith and Mr and Mrs Franklin.

William Smith's father was then called. He said,

> "I live at a distance of five or seven minutes walk from my son's cottage. I walked past my son's cottage at about half past four on the way to my Master's field. I saw my son at his water pump, and remember wishing him a good morning. I returned from my Master's field at about five, I saw my son at his door".

Coroner Poole seems to have been bedevilled by witnesses who needed to be recalled. The next was Mr George Mann, Governor of Coventry Jail. He said that on 1st June he was present at the enquiry and outside the room Mann had remarked that Smith 'has a long job in front of him'. Franklin replied, 'Yes, he has. He is the man that shot Owen'. Mann asked how he knew and was told, 'I was in the road and saw him shoot Owen. If I had been examined I would have told the Coroner all about it, I would have mentioned this before, but I thought I would get seven years transportation for being present'.

William Smith junior was then recalled and denied asking Mrs Franklin to state the time he had left their house on the morning of the murder.

The taking of evidence paused while discussion took place between the Coroner and the Rev Lickorish, a County Magistrate. The Coroner wanted Franklin to make an oral statement and this was eventually agreed, but it had first to be explained to Franklin that he need not do so.

John Franklin agreed to speak and told of drinking with William Smith and Eli Stretton at the Blacksmith's Arms in Ryton until about 11.45 pm, and of Smith accompanying him home. They had sat talking till about 1.30 when the Leicester Butcher called and left some meat

[There seems no reason to have made this up, and Smith said the same. But what in the world is going on? No one goes to bed and butchers sell meat in the middle of the night.]

Franklin said that his wife had cooked some of the mutton and the three had eaten, finishing at about half 2.30 am. Smith had a bottle with three pints of ale, which they drank with supper.

After eating Franklin had slept for about an hour, waking when Smith threw the empty beer bottle against the wall.

"I looked up at the clock when I woke up, it was half past three in the morning. My wife and Smith were in the room. My wife said that she was tired and that she would sit up no longer, she then went to bed.

Smith talked about going, and said, 'Come along with me and bring your gun'. It was five in the morning by my clock when we left, my clock was an hour and a quarter too fast this would make the correct time about 3.45. Neither man had guns.

Franklin had been going to his brother in law's, but Smith said, 'Come with me, I've got a gun in the lane, and we can shoot a rabbit'.

"We went on until we reached a culvert, not far from Mr Bagshaw's Barn, Smith pulled out a gun .... When we were up at the top of the field near the Toll Gate, I turned round and saw Joseph Owen coming along the path we had followed. At this time Smith was about a hundred yards or so in front of me, I shouted to him, 'Here's our Looker Outer a coming'. Smith said,

'Never mind, I won't be done by no Looker Outer'. We then went on until we got to the Oxford road, I was then about two fields from Askew's garden, and one field from the crossroad.

When we got to the road, Smith was about twenty yards in front of me, and Owen was close behind him. I beckoned to Owen, I thought that if Owen came up to me, Smith would get away with the gun, but Owen carried on after Smith and ignored me.

When Smith got onto the Oxford road, he went two yards or so in the direction of Coventry, and stood on the grass. Owen was in the middle of the road, and they appeared to be about five yards apart. I was then about a hundred yards away from them. I heard Smith say, 'I won't be done, I'll shoot first', he then pulled the gun from his pocket, and for a minute or so they walked in the direction of Coventry. I heard Owen say, 'Shoot then', and Smith fired the gun, Owen fell immediately.

I ran back to the gate of the field, and Smith ran back to the stile, this was between half past four and five in the morning, by the right time. We both went on down two fields, and met at a gate at the bottom of the second field, I said, 'What did you do that for Bill?', he replied, 'Oh be damned, it's done, and it can't be undone'.

We .... got out onto the Bubbenhall road, where we parted company. Smith threatened me before we parted that if I ever told anyone, he would shoot me if he got the chance. I then went home, and as soon as I got there I looked at my clock, it was a quarter past six, it was five a clock by the time of day. I saw nobody from the time I left Smith till I got to my own cottage. After remaining at home for about half an hour, I went about a hundred yards in the direction of the spot where the murder was committed, and then I returned home, and met old Samuel Smith on the way".

The Coroner remarked that Smith was taller than Owen and that when the shot was fired the muzzle of the gun was about a yard from Owen's ear. Franklin then went on to tell of borrowing a gun from his sister about three months previously, with one charge of powder, and one or two charges of shot.

"I cannot say whether this gun was the one with which the murder was committed .... I believe my wife found the gun, and hid it away, she would not tell me what she had done with it. On the Sunday evening when Smith came to my cottage, we agreed to say that he had left my cottage at half past two that morning."

The hearing was briefly adjourned after which the Coroner asked Smith if he would like to ask Franklin any questions. Smith merely said that Franklin had not told one word of truth, provoking an argument with Franklin which the Coroner cut short.

Eliza Smith was examined next. She said that between 3.00 and 4.00 on the morning of the murder her husband had came home. He had no gun with him when he had left home the previous night, he fired a gun which he had borrowed a short time after getting home He had no other gun except that one

> "I called with my husband at Franklin's cottage on the evening of the murder. Mrs Franklin told me that her husband left them between two and three that morning. I did not ask Mrs Franklin to say my husband had left their cottage that morning at half past two".

Joseph Perkins, the shoemaker who had lent his gun to Franklin some 12 months previously, was called to give further evidence.

> "I was asked by Mrs Smith to go to Franklin's, to tell Franklin to say to the Police what they had agreed to say the previous Sunday night".

He delivered the message accordingly. Mrs Franklin said that it would be very unnatural for her to say anything to Mrs Smith that would have the effect of getting her husband into trouble. The Coroner said that because to some extent new light had been thrown on to the matter, he deemed it necessary to adjourn to Wednesday, 23rd June.

23rd June - Last Hearing

The sixth session of this marathon inquest was at the Blacksmith's Arms, but this time it was held outside under the spreading branches of a fine chestnut tree. The pub yard was enclosed to keep the crowds back. John Franklin was brought up looking 'pale and anxious, but appeared perfectly self possessed'. Ann Franklin, his wife was recalled. She said,

> "On the morning of the murder when the witness Smith was at our cottage, he said to my husband, 'Jack don't go to sleep, if you do I'll shoot you, for I've got a pistol in my pocket'".

The long and confusing enquiry drew to a close and the Coroner summed up the evidence. He told the Jury that they had to decide between the statements of Franklin and Smith. If they believed Franklin then they could only arrive at the conclusion that Smith was the murderer. On the other hand, if they believed Smith they could scarcely hesitate to say that the crime was committed by Franklin.

They had no right to infer that the murder was committed while the two were together. It was as likely that the men parted company before the shot was fired as afterwards.

The Coroner did not think it necessary for the Jury to say what time the men left Franklin's house. He was disposed to believe Franklin's wife in this respect, that they probably went out at half past three, which would still leave time to commit the murder.

After that sensible beginning to making sense of the tangle of evidence, the Coroner pointed out the testimony to corroborate the time Smith had reached home.

He referred at considerable length to the discrepancies and improbabilities in the statements of Franklin and his wife, observing that if they were to be believed, Smith must have been carrying the gun given to him by Mrs Franklin, the beer and a pistol.

Trying to forge some conclusions from all the statements, the Coroner suggested that Smith went out on the Saturday night with the intention of getting some beer to take home; that he met Franklin at the Blacksmith's Arms and was induced to stay out much later than he intended.

He thought it a 'circumstance of grave suspicion' against Franklin that the gun which had been lent him by the Hobdays was not produced. The fact that Franklin had hidden the gun seemed to show that there was some mystery about it. He referred to the falsehoods told by Franklin to the Chief Constable when he was first arrested, but added that it was a very common thing for innocent people who felt themselves under suspicion to tell falsehoods, with the view of screening themselves. The Jury must not take the fact that these mis-statements were made alone, but in conjunction with other facts.

The Coroner left to the last the gravest question of all, the motive for the murder. There was a motive which might apply to Franklin, but could not apply to Smith. Franklin rented a cottage at a very low rent. His wife had been told that if her husband was seen poaching or carrying firearms they would be turned out. Owen had obviously seen Franklin carrying a gun. This was a motive for someone in Franklin's position to silence Owen, and he might in a fit of temper have shot him. The Coroner did not seem to believe that avoiding arrest and imprisonment or transportation might be a motive for murder. Having prejudiced Franklin's case, he told the Jury to consider their verdict.

The Jury had no sooner retired than they were brought back to hear yet more evidence from a man called Thomas Poultney. At about 4.30 on the morning of the murder he said that he was going from Coventry to Southam and met Franklin and Smith near the Bull & Butcher public house. Smith had a gun in his hand. They were walking towards Coventry. Just after passing Poultney they crossed the road and went into a field on the left hand side. Poultney pointed to Franklin and Smith to identify them as the people he had seen and pointing to Franklin said, 'He cannot deny it because he saw me at the time'. He heard the clock strike 4.00 when he was at Willenhall. He had left Foleshill at 2.00 am and had walked steadily. Smith was wearing a dark shooting coat, such as poachers wear.

After Smith and Franklin had passed him Poultney had heard Smith say, 'I won't be done, let who will come'. When he passed the Bull & Butcher he had seen a man in the field who appeared to be moving away from him.

He explained his late appearance in the case:

"I have attended here every day of the inquest and have been pushed back whenever I attempted to get into the room". He had seen the Jurymen go away on that morning and said to the people around the house, "I am determined to speak today of what I know".

The Coroner pressed Poultney closely and cross examined him at great length. Poultney admitted that he had been in prison for 'being with a man who stole a waistcoat'. He claimed to be well acquainted with Smith and Franklin, but a police officer proved that as soon as Poultney had arrived that morning, he had asked, 'Which is the prisoner? Which is Franklin?'.

William Hewitt was called, and said that he had seen Poultney on the road that morning, and the latter had enquired the way to Marton. Hewitt had directed him, but he had observed that Poultney was heading towards Ryton. Poultney then said, 'Oh, it's Ryton, I mean, I want to go to the inquest'.

Poultney was questioned again. He said it was on the morning of Monday, 10th May, that he had seen Smith and Franklin, and not Sunday the 9th as previously stated. This statement caused 'great excitement' amongst the people around the house. The Coroner told Poultney that he did not believe a word he had said, that if he escaped he may think himself lucky, but he was very liable to be prosecuted for perjury.

The Jury retired for about 45 minutes, then returned with a verdict of 'Wilful Murder against some person or persons unknown'. This appeared to be generally accepted by all present, but Poultney's attempt at perjury had caused such resentment in the crowd that he was forced to run away.

John Franklin, unnamed by the Coroner's Jury despite the Coroner's efforts, was still on remand to the Magistrates' Court at Warwick County Hall. When his case was first heard the inquest evidence that related to him was read out and the Magistrates committed him for trial at the Assizes.

In those days Assize Courts did not simply accept cases for trial by committal from Magistrates Courts, as Crown Courts now do. At the beginning of each Assize a Grand Jury sat to review the evidence against each prisoner and decide whether it was sufficient to found a case for trial. If it did they presented a Bill of Indictment. This duplication of effort continued until the 1940s. There is a door in Birmingham's Victoria Law Courts which still bears the name 'Grand Jury Room'.

On 6th August 1858 the Grand Jury at Warwick declared No True Bill against John Franklin, that is, there was not enough evidence for a Bill. Mr Elers, who was instructed to defend Franklin, applied to the Judge for his client's discharge. Mr

Justice Wightman asked if the prisoner was charged on the Coroners Inquisition. This was an alternative way of obtaining an Indictment.

Mr Elers replied 'No my lord, the Jury returned an open verdict'. Mr Justice Wightman then said 'Let the prisoner be liberated', and Franklin was discharged.

Despite the Coroner's belief that the killer was either Franklin or Smith, no other arrest was ever made for the murder of Joseph Owen.

You must make up your own minds, because we shall never know.

✳ ✳ ✳

There is a grim little footnote to all this. In *Midland Murders & Mysteries* we published a story called 'This Unfortunate Woman', about a woman murdered on a canal boat at Rugeley in 1839. The captain and another man were hanged for it and the captain's name was James Owen. He was a cousin of Joseph Owen and great uncle of Gary Moore, who first told this tale.

'A cure for the rankish itch.'
(Burntwood, Staffs 1843)

Sarah Westwood was the wife of John Westwood, a nailmaker
at Burntwood in Staffordshire. In 1843 he was 40 and she 42.
They had been married for twenty years and, apart from an
illegitimate child of Sarah's from before her marriage, had
seven children. Three of their offspring had left home but
one son, Charles, who worked with his father, and four
little girls remained at home.

Lodging in the Westwood's home for six or seven years was a
Samuel Phillips, and about harvest time of 1843, a neighbour
came across Phillips and Westwood struggling on the ground
in a lane. Sarah stood by and was encouraging Phillips with
cries of 'Kill him!. Her husband was heard to demand of
Phillips, 'Damn your eyes! What was you doing at her
when I knocked you down?'

When victory went to her husband, Sarah shouted that she
would leave him and beg her bread from door to door.

Shortly afterwards a row broke out between the couple when
they were at the home of Robert Westwood, John's brother.
John accused Phillips and Sarah of stealing some ale, which
Sarah denied. Her husband ordered her to stop going out with
Phillips, but she refused and swore at him.

In country areas at that time, every hand in the village was
turned to reaping at harvest time. Women played as big a part
as men, walking behind the reapers and bundling the corn into
sheaves. That night Sarah refused to go home with John, sitting
all night by Robert Westwood's fire and complaining that, 'It's
hard work to go out reaping and have to sit by the fire'.

Robert Westwood also saw another dispute, when John invited
Sarah to go 'a-tea drinking' at the Bell Inn. Sarah refused and
John replied, 'If I hadn't wanted to have gone you'd have been
there. Recollect you wanted to make a child of me by locking
the door last night'.

Harvest time passed, but it seems that relations between John
and Sarah did not improve. On 9th November 1843 John and
his son spent the morning working together, after which John
complained of feeling starved. Astonishingly, Samuel Phillips

was still lodging there but was not at home, so John, Sarah, Charles and the three little girls ate together. John had gruel with sugar and butter, some meat and fried bread. Eliza Westwood, aged 10, remembered hearing him ask her mother what was the white substance mixed in his gruel and Sarah replying that she did not know.

Lunch over, Charles returned to work, but John read a few pages of the Bible then went to rest on his bed, something he had done after recovering from typhus a year before.

In the late afternoon John began to vomit. About 8.00 pm Charles heard his mother ask whether she should send for a doctor. John refused, saying that he would be alright if he could only get warm, but an hour later he was dead.

The dead man's family voiced some suspicions and there was a postmortem, then Sarah was arrested and committed for trial. The hearing opened at Stafford Assizes on 28th December 1843.

Samuel Phillips's mother was Hannah Mason, a 'wise woman', that is, a herbalist or folk healer. She said in evidence that Sarah had come to her home in Walsall on 1st November and asked if Hannah knew how to cure 'the itch'. They had gone together to a chemist's shop, where Hannah bought hellebore, arsenic and red and white precipitate. She had mixed them with her fingers, while in the shop, and had told Sarah that the mixture would 'cure the rankish itch in twenty four hours by wearing the linen for a fortnight '(sic).

Sarah's children had said that no one in the house was suffering from the itch, but on 8th November, the day before John's death, Sarah had returned to the chemist's shop in Walsall. She was alone, but the chemist knew Hannah Mason well and sold her the ingredients for the ointment.

A doctor deposed that John Westwood's stomach had contained a huge amount of arsenic, between a quarter and half an ounce.

The Jury had no difficulty in finding Sarah guilty, though they recommended mercy. Judge's disliked recommendations to mercy for poisoners and she was sentenced to death. Pleading pregnancy as a reason for a reprieve, she was examined by a jury of matrons appointed by the Court. They found that she was not pregnant, and she was hanged at Stafford on 13th January 1844. It seemed that no one was curious about the fact that it was Phillips's mother who showed Sarah how to get arsenic.

'Oh God! Is it my wife?'
(Walsall & Cannock Chase 1964 - 1969)

If the first incident did not end in murder it was not the killer's fault. He had left his victim raped and choked in a ditch, believing her dead. It was a black, wet December night in 1964, when the cold seeped into the bones. That the victim did not die was the work of chance.

A cyclist, head down no doubt in the bitter night, heard a moaning sound from a ditch at Bentley in the northern part of Walsall. Despite the weather he stopped to investigate and found a 9 year old girl. She had been lured away from her home less than an hour before, savagely assaulted, strangled and flung into a ditch. A very little more time, minutes perhaps, and the crime would have been murder.

The child could tell the Police only that she had been abducted by a man who called himself 'Uncle Len'. He told her that he had been sent by her mother to take her to her aunt's to collect Christmas presents.

A witness had seen a car beside the ditch where she was found. It was a grey Vauxhall Cresta with tailfins and a quite unusual feature, a hand spotlamp fixed at the driver's end of the windscreen.

An Identikit portrait was constructed and widely circulated on posters. Every effort was made to trace that grey car, but a year passed without an arrest.

On Wednesday 8th September 1965 another child was lured away. Margaret Reynolds, nearly 7, left her home in Clifton Road, Aston, Birmingham with her sister to return to school after lunch. She was carrying a green toy umbrella. Her sister attended a different school, so they separated and Margaret vanished completely. There were no clues, so no link was made at the time with the Walsall case, but the police explored another possibility.

Manchester Police were investigating the disappearances of a number of children, which were finally laid at the door of Ian Brady and Myra Hindley, the so called 'Moors Murderers'. Birmingham officers exchanged information with their northern colleagues, but it brought no result.

On Thursday 30th December another child disappeared, this time from Walsall. Diane Joy Tift was reported missing at 7 pm. but no one had actually seen her since early afternoon. By New Year's Day she was still not found and Walsall Police called on the assistance of the newly created Regional Crime Squads in Stoke on Trent, Birmingham and Wolverhampton.

There was little to tell when they arrived in Walsall. Diane lived in Hollemeadow Avenue, Bloxwich. She had been at her grandmother's in Chapel Street and left about 1.30 or 2.00 pm. There was an inconclusive sighting of her passing a nearby launderette and she might have made for a shopping precinct to play, but she had not been seen since.

Diane's clothing was described and Crime Squad officers were shown a pink plastic handbag with white diamond decorations like the one she had been carrying. Walsall officers had made a massive house to house enquiry but found no one who could report any further sightings. They had searched wasteland and dragged pools and canals without finding her. Now they asked the Crime Squad teams to search every house and outbuilding on the huge estate where Diane lived.

Six thousand homes were searched, not to mention garages, garden sheds and derelict factories. One policeman recalled the magnificent cooperation of the local people who allowed them to search without warrants, remembering that only one citizen, a Walsall County Borough Councillor and member of the Watch Committee, refused them access. In the course of the search he recalls that they found enough evidence of other crimes to 'have filled the cells in Walsall and Bloxwich, and we could have given Walsall CID a bonanza', but they did not. People had cooperated and the searchers turned a blind eye where necessary.

Whatever the searchers did find they found no clue to Diane's disappearance and the Regional Crime Squad men dispersed, leaving Walsall CID to continue the hunt. They had not been gone long when on 12th January they were recalled, together with CID officers from all over the area. Diane Tift's body had been found.

Cannock Chase lies some 10 miles north of Walsall, a sand and gravel plateau of some 26 square miles covered by conifer forest and heathland. It is a playground for the nearby industrial towns. Walkers, picnickers, cyclists, horse riders, lovers, botanists,

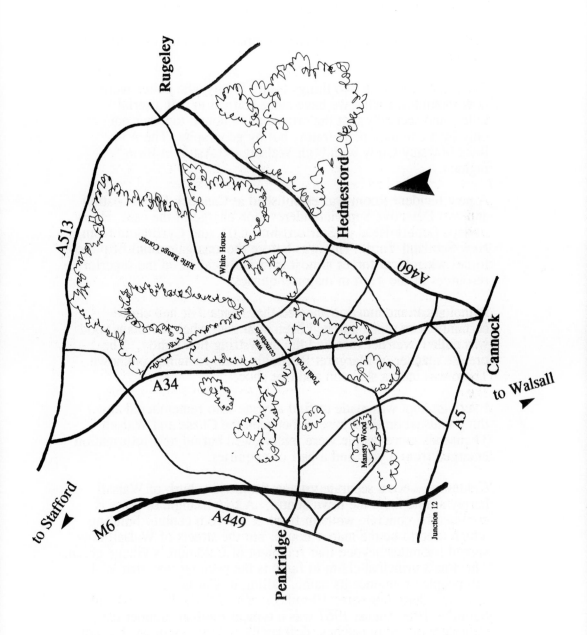

Rugeley

Hednesford

A460

Cannock

to Walsall

A513

Rifle Range Corner

White House

A34

War commemorates

Pool Pool

Mansty Wood

A5

Junction 12

to Stafford

M6

A449

Penkridge

bird watchers, artists, joggers - all manner of people use the Chase.

The M6 runs parallel with its western edge at a distance of some 2.5 miles. The A34 runs in the same direction but less than a mile away. The Penkridge to Rugeley road joins the two, and just south of it lies Manstey Gully. Here Diane's body was found, together with the badly decomposed remains of Margaret Reynolds.

The discovery made two things clear. Firstly, the police were now looking for what we have since learned to call a serial killer, and secondly that the crimes were bound together not only by a common perpetrator, but by geography. The A34 links Manstey Gully with both Walsall and Aston in Birmingham.

A new Incident Room was established at Cannock Police Station and two Detective Superintendents took charge of the case, Harry Bailey, Deputy Head of Staffordshire CID, and Cyril Gold from New Scotland Yard. This was before the amalgamations of police forces when local forces almost invariably called on the superior resources of the Yard in major enquiries.

Pathological examination showed that Diane Tift had almost certainly been raped and had been strangled when her pixie hood was pulled over her face and the drawstring tied tightly. The precise manner of Margaret Reynolds death remained unknown. There was only a skeleton and one shoe.

Every attempt was made to find anyone who remembered anything unusual on the Chase or between the Chase and Walsall. Thousands more people were interviewed but no new information emerged from a year and a half of enquiries.

Caldmore, once a separate village, is now a suburb of Walsall barely a mile from the town centre. A tiny triangle of grass is confined by concrete walls in front of the 16th century building which used to be the manor house, but the streets of Walsall now spread for miles beyond that fragment of Caldmore's village green. The area's principal claim to fame is the peculiar way that Walsall people pronounce its name, calling it 'Carmer'.

Saturday 19th August 1967 was a typical English summer day, a mixture of sunny patches, dull spells and rain showers, but not wet enough to drive children indoors. At about 2.30 pm 7 year old Christine Darby was one of a group of children playing near her home in Camden Street, Caldmore. They were near Corporation Street, which climbs a slight hill from the Wednesbury Road to Caldmore Green, when a car stopped beside them.

The driver wound down the passenger's window and asked the children, 'Could you show me the way to Caldmore Green, please?' All of the children said, 'Up that way' and pointed up the hill. The man opened the passenger door and asked Christine, 'Could you get in and show me the way, please?'

Christine got into the car and closed the door. The driver backed up onto Corporation Street and turned towards the Wednesbury Road traffic lights. Instantly Christine's playmates realised that something was amiss. The car had gone the wrong way, not towards Caldmore Green. They ran to tell Mrs Darby what had happened.

After the discovery of the bodies at Manstey Gully, the Staffordshire, West Midlands and Birmingham Police forces had created a 'Stop Plan' for any future abduction. Immediately they heard of a missing child they would seal the area of the abduction, block important main roads and establish a police presence on all access roads around Cannock Chase. This now came into operation, but time and distance were against them. It was about 20 minutes after the abduction before the Police knew, far more than the time necessary to drive from Caldmore to the Chase.

The Stop Plan had failed, but the police had some advantages over the previous cases. In Christine's playmate, 8 year old Nicholas Baldry, they had a good witness. He could describe the car driver; in his 30s, darkish hair, clean shaven, fairly thin, wearing a white shirt with no tie. About the car he was less certain. It was light grey and he thought it was like the Ford Consul that parked in his street. He was sure, however, that the man had asked for 'Carmer Green'. Now the police knew they were looking for a Walsall man.

There was other evidence as well. A grey car had been seen hanging about a local primary school for the past fortnight, and a grey Morris Oxford was noticed in Camden Street while the children played that afternoon between 2.15 and 2.30. Other sightings indicated another journey to the Chase.

You have seen police searches for missing children on television, a line of officers at fingertip distance moving steadily across a piece of ground. It works very well, but you can't do it across an area some 13 miles long by 9 miles wide pitted with derelict mineshafts, particularly not when a large part of it is covered by the gloomy density of Forestry Commission plantations, and especially not in August when the heather and bracken over the rest of the Chase is at its highest. Nevertheless, the Chase had to be searched.

This view of a hilly part in the north of Cannock Chase shows how difficult a full search would be.

Sunday 20th August 1967 dawned clear and sunny, and the first attempt at searching began as six mounted officers moved in a line eastwards from the A34. PC Ellis was moving along the Penkridge to Rugeley road and was not far east of Pottal Pool crossroads when he spotted a piece of cloth hanging in a fallen tree north of the road. It was a child's panties, and Christine Darby's grandmother was able to identify her own mending on them.

There was now an indication that narrowed the search and relieved those senior officers who had been estimating that five hundred men would take three months to search the Chase. On Monday the Chief Constable of Staffordshire, Arthur Morgan Rees, assembled three hundred officers at Pottal Pool crossroads and launched them eastwards in a search line, two arm's lengths apart. Each tenth man in the line unrolled a ball of string as he moved, fixing it to trees and bushes, so as to indicate the cleared areas. Before the operation ended, seven hundred and fifty officers were involved and 14 miles of string had been unwound.

At 1.00 pm there was another find. A forestry worker moving through woodland north of the Pentridge to Rugely road found a child's plimsoll lying in bracken close to the road, about 3 miles east of the search line. Henrietta Darby identified it as her grandchild's shoe.

At twilight the search stopped, to begin again on Tuesday with more than twice as many searchers. Five hundred policemen had been augmented by some fifty Royal Air Force men from RAF Stafford and two hundred troops from the Staffordshire Regiment at Whittington Barracks. The long line pressed steadily east from 8.00 until 5.00 pm, when the police called a halt intending to stop for the day.

The Army were still keen and Major Nesbitt suggested that the remaining hours of daylight should be used to search Forestry Commission Plantation 110, which lay north of the White House where the line had halted. That, he thought, would give them a better start line the next morning.

The line moved off again. Three quarters of an hour later Private Blundred called out and lifted a hand. A whistle shrieked and the entire line stopped. Private Blundred had found Christine Darby's body.

When the Stop Plan had failed Chief Constable Rees was certain he had a murder in his jurisdiction. He called Scotland Yard so promptly that Detective Superintendent Ian Forbes arrived in Stafford on the evening that Christine Darby's corpse was found. Harry Bailey had contacted Alan Usher, who ran the Forensic Pathology Department at Sheffield University, and he was soon in Cannock.

Forestry plantations are unnatural places in broad daylight, with their rows of dark trees and their long, straight fire breaks and rides. Now, with midnight approaching, arc lamps lit the black heart of Plantation 110 and the policemen and Dr Usher set about their work in the weird green glow. Soon Dr Usher was able to confirm that Christine had been violently sexually assaulted and strangled, most probably on the day she was abducted.

Now there were new searches to be made, more door to door enquiries in Walsall, a fingertip search of the ground round the body, and a search for everyone who had been on Cannock Chase during that Saturday afternoon.

The ground search revealed tyre marks in the ride near to the body, impressed at intervals from the edge of the plantation to about 140 yards down the ride. They were not the marks of a heavy Forestry Commission vehicle and Mr Joseph Wilson, Technical Manager of Pirelli Tyres was asked to assist the police as he had done before. He could confirm that they were the tracks of a family saloon, that the driver was experienced enough to reverse out without making new tracks and that only one car had been in the ride since it rained on Saturday.

One after another, people who had visited the Chase that after-noon were interviewed and details of any vehicle they had used collected. They were asked about other people and vehicles they had seen, then they were traced and interviewed. Pins on a large plan of the Chase built up a picture of who was where and when. Six hundred pins soon revealed a suspicious car near Plantation 110, not a grey saloon, but a blue Volkswagen.

Two mushroom pickers had seen a man emerge from the ride near where the body was found and drive off in a blue Volkswagen at about 4.00 on the Saturday afternoon. Thousands of leaflets had been circulated and posters displayed, and the police hunt was daily in the press and on television. Why had the driver not come forward?

Enquiries with Volkswagen dealers and listings of registration number permutations eventually led the police to Victor White-house at Hednesford, whose home was on the edge of the Chase and virtually within sight of Plantation 110. For twenty years he had walked the Chase and freely admitted that he had been there on 19th August. He must have had some bad moments when the police demanded the reason for his silence, but he had one. He had not come forward because he didn't think that he was in their target area, and that was because the published plan of the Chase had the site of Christine's body marked in the wrong place.

If they had not found a suspect, the police had found a valuable witness because he had seen another vehicle backed into a ride, a grey car:

> "I remember the radiator grill was the full width of the car and it had a mesh grill. I am not absolutely satisfied about this, but if I was allowed to give this some thought and see several types of cars I think I would recognise it."

Austins, Fords, Morrises, Standards and Vauxhalls were put in the ride while he examined them. Finally he plumped for a light grey Austin A55 or A60 Farina. but he could remember nothing of its number.

He could, though, describe the driver, a man about 5'10" high, around 40 years old, smooth complexioned and ruddy, or flushed, with dark hair which was short or brushed back. He wore a dark jacket or blazer.

> "As I got nearer he moved towards the front of the car and I saw him full face," said Victor Whitehouse. "He looked at me. I think I would recognise him again if I saw him."

On the very same day another witness emerged. Mrs Jeanne Rawlings and her husband had picnicked near Plantation 110 on August 19th. While her husband delved in their car's boot, she had seen a vehicle come slowly down the side of the plantation, from the point where Victor Whitehouse must have seen it. She had no problem in identifying it, for her father had the same make and model. It was a light grey Austin A60 Farina saloon.

Jeanne Rawlings and Victor Whitehouse helped the police to create Identikit pictures of the car's driver, both very similar, and a *Birmingham Evening Mail* artist fleshed out the picture with colour. Soon the face and the details of the car were familiar to every newspaper reader and television watcher in Britain.

Information poured into the two Incident Rooms at Walsall and Cannock, now staffed by a hundred officers and linked by landlines and closed circuit TV. But there was a huge amount of sheer donkey work to be done in tracing that car among some forty five thousand Farinas in Britain.

January 1968 brought a new initiative by the police team. Convinced by the abductor's pronunciation of 'Caldmore' that he was a local man, they launched a house to house enquiry bigger than any ever carried out before. As snow swept the West Midlands, officers set out to call at every home in Walsall, completing a checklist of every occupant and asking every male between the ages of twenty one and fifty to account for his whereabouts on the day of the three murders. Not everyone who had been in Walsall on those dates was still there. Enquiries spread all over the world. A friend of the writer's was interviewed in the Middle East, while the police in Accra, Ghana, cabled Cannock that their officers believed that a suspect resembled the Identikit and had taken him into custody.

By early summer, nearly every one of Walsall's sixty four thousand homes had been visited. Every male had been interviewed apart from a few hundred who had left lodgings, or otherwise departed with no forwarding address. All but ten thousand Farinas had been traced, but ten thousand is a lot of cars.

At 4.30 pm on Saturday 21st May a phone call told Walsall Police that two small girls had been abducted from Stag Crescent, Bloxwich. A carefully noted car number now gave a chance for the Stop Plan to prove itself. In less than 10 minutes it was in place and in less than an hour a car was stopped at Aldridge, 5 miles from Walsall. Inside were the two little girls unharmed. The driver told police that they were the daughters of friends of his, but the girls disagreed and accused him of gagging them with sticking plaster and indecently assaulting then. While the West Midlands and the police held their breath, he was interrogated at Aldridge Police Station and eventually charged with indecent assault. He was not the A34 murderer.

When that man appeared in Aldridge Magistrates' Court, an angry crowd surrounded the court, yelling, 'Hang him!' Walsall people were angry, fearful and tired of the long hunt with no apparent results. As the police continued their trudge from door to door asking seemingly irrelevant questions and embarrassing men who had been where they shouldn't on one of the key dates, a fantastic theory was muttered angrily in pubs from end to end of the town. The A34 murderer, people said, was a policeman, and the police knew this and were concealing him.

In August 1968, twelve months after he came to the Midlands, Scotland Yard withdrew Ian Forbes and his Sergeant from the enquiry. The Incident Rooms continued to process information, though with reduced manpower, the last Farinas were being traced, but there was still no break in the case. Autumn was coming and it would soon be four years since the first victim was found half dead in Bentley.

The eve of Guy Fawkes' Night on 4th November saw children out on the streets collecting money for fireworks and building bonfires. On Bridgeman Street, close to Walsall's town centre, a car driver stopped his car that evening and asked a 10 year old girl who was building a bonfire on some wasteground, 'Do you want some fireworks? Do you want any rockets or catherine wheels?' When she said 'Yes', he pointed to his car and said, 'The fireworks are over there', opening the door and pointing.

She saw no fireworks, only a rear seat covered with newspaper and she made to move away. He took her arm and said, 'I'll open the door for you'. She broke free and moved away as he went round to the nearside of the car.

Wendy Lane aged 19 was leaving a nearby chip shop and had seen the incident. Now as the car drove away with the man bent over the wheel to conceal his face, she struggled to remember the registration number.

The police were not, at first, very excited. Apart from the Aldridge incident there had been many other attempted abductions in the Walsall area in four years that were not the work of the killer.

Wendy Lane believed the car was a green Ford Zephyr with a white roof, and that its number was 429 LOP. There was no Zephyr of that number, but trying permutations and showing Wendy pictures of cars produced the suggestion that it was a Ford Corsair. There was a Corsair, green with a white roof, registered to a man who lived in Regent House, a block of flats across the street from Walsall Police Station. Its number was 492 LOP.

Next day the car owner was taken to Walsall Police Station. He asked for a solicitor and named the lawyer who did most of the local prosecutions. He was put on an identity parade but was not identified. The police let him go.

Two officers from the Cannock Incident Room had been present at Walsall as a matter of routine. They were astonished by the resemblance between the suspect and the Identikit picture and more so when they learned that his previous vehicle had been a grey A55.

It emerged that the suspect had been interviewed a month after the last murder, as the owner of an A55. He had been alibied only by his wife. Excitement growing, officers at Cannock and Walsall began to cross refer everything they knew that might bear on this man. Next they discovered that he had been interviewed again in February 1968, in the big door to door enquiry. His witness form from that enquiry had been filed at Walsall while his form from the car enquiry was at Cannock.

There had also been an interview in October 1966 when two little girls had complained about a man who had invited them to his flat in Regenct House. He paid them two shillings (10p) each to allow him to take photographs of them in their knickers with his hand on their private parts. His flat had been searched and photographic equipment found, but he denied the allegations and the complaint had not been made until some time afterwards. The West Midlands Prosecuting Solicitor decided not to proceed against him. Nobody had told the Incident Room of the case.

Suspicion went even further back, all the way to January 1966 when the bodies of Margaret Reynolds and Diane Tift were found at Manstey Gully. In the wake of that discovery a member of the public had visited Cannock Police Station and made a statement of his suspicions that his own brother was the killer. He had no proof to offer, only his suspicions, but it might have counted in the balance if it had been cross indexed under his name and his brother's. In fact, it was indexed only under the informant's name and so ignored until someone remembered it.

By 14th November Ian Forbes had been called back from the Yard and a plan was in place. At 7.15 on Friday 15th November a police officer stopped the suspect outside Regent House to make a 'routine check' on his driving licence. Moments later Detective Chief Inspector Molloy, Detective Inspector Norman Williams and Detective Constable Conrad Joseph moved in and arrested the driver on suspicion of the murder of Christine Darby. 'Oh God!' he exclaimed, 'Is it my wife?'

As their suspect languished in a cell at Stafford, Molloy and Forbes interviewed his wife that afternoon at Hednesford Police

Station. She had originally said that her husband had arrived home at about 2.00 pm on 19th August 1967 and that they had gone to her parents' home. She had relied entirely on her husband's recollection of events. Now at last she remembered that when her husband had arrived home, she had gone to Marks & Spencer in Walsall to buy some cakes which her mother wanted. When she got there they were about to close, it must have been much later than 2.00. Her parents, who had never been questioned before, recalled that their visitors had arrived just after the football results ended at about 5.15 and their son in law said that he had been late leaving work that afternoon.

This new information was put to the suspect during an interview on Friday evening, but he still made no admissions and refused to take part in an identity parade. He was asked again next morning but again refused. Taken to the yard of the Police Station, he was confronted by Victor Whitehouse who confirmed that this was the man he had seen on Cannock Chase.

At 12.15 pm at Cannock, Ian Forbes read the charge to the suspect:

"Raymond Leslie Morris, I charge you that on or about the 19th day of August 1968 in the County of Stafford, you did murder Christine Anne Darby, Contrary to Common Law."

Chief Inspector Molloy in his book, *The Cannock Chase Murders* (Gomer Press 1988, NEL 1990) makes much of the luck, good or bad, that attended the long enquiry. He does his colleagues less than justice. 'Diligence makes its own good fortune', says the proverb, and when Morris at last fell into Police hands they knew how to put together a case against him because they had done their homework. But one has to wonder whether he would not have been arrested earlier if the handling of information in the enquiry had been more careful and the checking of alibis more thorough.

When Morris' flat was searched a set of indecent photographs of a little girl were found. They turned out to be pictures of his niece, who lived in Wales but had spent short holidays at the flat in the summers of 1967 and 1968. The pictures had been taken on the second occasion. In December he was charged with three more offences, the attempted abduction from Bridgeman Street and two indecent assaults on his niece.

Morris was committed from Cannock Magistrates' Court in January 1969 to stand trial at Stafford Assizes. On February 10th the trial began.

The Defence sought to separate the charge of murder from those of indecent assaults on the basis that the evidence in the assaults would hopelessly prejudice the trial of the murder. Morris pleaded guilty to the assaults, but the Prosecution argued that evidence of them was 'similar fact' evidence.

Normally when someone is tried for, say, theft, the prosecution will not be allowed to bring evidence linking the accused with an attack on someone in a separate incident. The issue is not whether they are generally a bad person who might steal things, but whether they committed the particular offence. There are plenty of other thieves about who might have done it. Even so, if the accused can be linked to traces of hot buttered toast at the scenes of both the attack and the theft, the judge might allow such evidence because the 'similar facts' will help to identify the accused, not just show that he is a bad lot.

The evidence of indecent assaults against Morris showed that he had a sexual interest in small girls, and this was as relevant in the murder trial as his physical appearance. The Judge ruled in favour of the Prosecution.

The Defence tried to weaken the evidence of the Prosecution's witnesses, with some successes, but they failed to shake Victor Whitehouse or Mrs Rawlings, both of whom were quite sure that it was Morris they saw on Cannock Chase on 19th August 1967.

Poor Mrs Carol Morris could not be compelled to give evidence against her husband but did so voluntarily. She was given a hard time by Kenneth Mynett QC, defence counsel, over her versions of her husband's movements:

Counsel: On three separate occasions you were not merely allowing it to be said in your presence but confirming that he was shopping with you?

Mrs Morris: I said that because I didn't think he was the person responsible.

Counsel: You believed at the time that what you were telling the police officers was the truth?

Mrs Morris: I believed it because I couldn't believe he was the person connected

The Judge, Mr Justice Ashworth, complained that he did not understand and Mrs Morris said she had known what she was saying was untrue, but she could not believe it.

Counsel: You have told us that you could not believe that your husband could have had anything to do with it?

Mrs Morris: Because he came home and had his meal and acted normally without any signs of emotion.

Her parents were unshakeable in their recollection that the Morris's had arrived at their home at about 5.15 pm. A clocking out card proved that Morris had left work at 1.13 pm that day. He had been missing for three hours before he actually arrived home. Chief Inspector Molloy was accused of hitting Morris during an interview, though Morris had made no admissions. It all mattered very little. There was clearly material on which a Jury could convict, unless the Defence could tell them why they should not.

At last Morris entered the witness box. He was being examined by his own counsel when a child's voice echoed from the public gallery above. 'That's him!' it cried, 'That's the man! Him down there!' Over the rail of the gallery a young girl was pointing at Morris.

It was the child who had been left for dead in a ditch at Bentley more than four years before. She was quickly ushered out of the gallery, where she should never have been. Morris had not been charged with that attack as only his ownership of a Cresta car connected him with it.

Morris gave evidence for more than four hours on that day and another two on the next. He insisted that the police questioning was wrongly recorded, that he had never been asked to stand on an ID parade and he repeated the accusations against DCh Insp Molloy. He tried to imply that the photographs of his niece arose because, while she was posing for him fully dressed she chose to take her clothes off. He wriggled about his movements on 19th August 1967 and wriggled harder when Prosecuting counsel made clear that the frame numbers on the negatives of his photos of his niece showed that he had lied about the sequence.

In his closing speech, Morris' counsel sought sympathy from the Jury:

> "We have no conception of the isolation which he feels having pleaded guilty to one horrible, dirty, offence and facing trial for murder - and murder of the worst and most revolting kind. His life, whatever the result is completely wrecked. He has been deserted by his wife, who has not only deserted him but voluntarily given evidence against him."

After seven days of evidence and the closing speeches of Prosecution and Defence the Judge began to sum up. He was scrupulous in his reminder that the photographs were merely part of the evidence of identification, he reminded the Jury that 1,998 cars had registrations containing the letters LOP but only one was a green and white Corsair. He warned them to treat Mrs Morris' evidence with care and to consider that she had either lied in her earlier answers to the police or she had lied in the witness box. He reminded them that Morris had said he only started using a carwash in Caldmore after Christine Darby's disappearance, but the carwash manager remembered him as a customer who came in at different times on Saturday afternoons around that time.

It took the Jury less than two hours to find guilty verdicts on both abduction and murder counts. The verdicts were cheered by the public gallery and a crowd in the square outside chanted 'Hang him! Hang him!' and 'Give him to us!', but they cheered Wendy Lane who had remembered the killer's car number on 4th November.

> "I am very pleased that he has been put out of the way," she said. "Only people living in the Walsall area know how frightened everyone has been."

Mr Justice Ashworth said:

> "There must be many mothers in Walsall and in the area whose hearts will beat more lightly as a result of this verdict."

Raymond Morris was sentenced to life imprisonment and his appeal was refused.

'Your time is come - you must die.'
(Staunton Harold, Leics 1760)

Watching the process of dismantling the House of Lords, or
removing its powers, or restructuring, or whatever is really
happening, you might forget one of its functions. Aside from
debating and law making, the House is the highest appeal court
in Britain. Something almost forgotten is that it was once a
court of first trial.

Laurence Shirley, Earl Ferrers suffered from an affliction common
amongst people with too much time and money and too few brains,
he was addicted to alcohol. Sober, he was an unremarkable example
of the 18th century English aristocracy (which gave wide enough
scope for eccentricity), 'when under the influence of intoxication
he acted with all the wildness and brutality of a madman'.

Marriage improves some people, but not the Earl. Wed in 1752
to the youngest daughter of Sir William Meredith, he behaved
himself for a while but soon reverted to his former self, treating
his wife with 'such unwarrantable cruelty that she was forced to
flee his house'.

Whether to make the Earl suffer a little or because he could not
afford to maintain his daughter in frocks and powder, Sir William
petitioned Parliament for a private Act. These only affect particular people or land and were used, for example, to create the
early railway and canal companies and grant them land purchase
powers. Occasionally they were used to get a divorce. Sir
William's Act gave his daughter a maintenance allowance
to be raised from her husband's estate.

Among the officers of Ferrers' estate was a steward called John
Johnson, a man 'remarkable only for the regularity of his manner,
the accuracy of his accounts, and his fidelity as a steward'. The
Earl was anxious that this man should take on the duty of receiving and paying over to Lady Ferrers certain rents which were
assigned to her. The appointment may have been made in the
belief that Johnson would be faithful to his master rather than
this duty. If so it was an error of judgement. Johnson seems to
have been aware of the dangerous possibilities of the post and
refused, but was prevailed upon by the Earl.

The Earl's household now consisted of himself, a Mrs Clifford, described in contemporary accounts as 'a lady who lived with him', her five daughters, five menservants, three maids, an old man and a boy. They lived at Staunton Harold, then known as Stanton, near Ashby de la Zouch, while John Johnson occupied a farmhouse called the Lount about half a mile away.

Johnson probably carried out his duties as the Countess' trustee as faithfully and accurately as he worked for the Earl. Within a fairly short time the Earl grew suspicious and accused him of causing the loss of a highly profitable coal contract. Accusations of conspiracy, treachery and dishonesty multiplied and the Earl tried to dismiss Johnson from his tenancy of the Lount.

The Act of Parliament which created his wife's trust may have forseen that Ferrers would attack the steward because it had granted him the lease of the Lount, so the Earl could not evict him. This probably sealed the fate of both Johnson and his master.

On Sunday 13th January 1760 Ferrers visited the Lount and commanded Johnson to attend on him at 3.00 pm on the following Friday. Before the appointment Ferrers told Mrs Clifford to take her daughters for a walk and return at 5.30, then sent his menservants on various errands. Johnson arrived at a house occupied only by the Earl and three maids.

The steward came on time. After a few minutes he was shown into the Earl's room, where Ferrers locked the door behind him. After a short conversation about an account, the Earl began abusing Johnson in a voice loud enough for the maids to hear through the locked door. They heard him cry, 'Down on your other knee! Declare you have acted against Lord Ferrers!' Johnson would not admit the accusation, so the Earl drew a loaded pistol from his pocket, crying, 'Your time is come, you must die!', and shot Johnson.

Despite his wound, Johnson stood up and asked the Earl to stop the attack. The maids arrived at the door, Lord Ferrers walked out, and a messenger was sent to fetch Mr Kirkland, a surgeon at Ashby de la Zouch.

Johnson was put to bed and Lord Ferrers enquired how he was. The steward said that he was dying and wished his family sent for. Miss Johnson soon arrived and Lord Ferrers now pulled down the injured man's bedclothes and applied to the wound

'a pledget dipped in arquebusade water', before leaving the room again.

[According to the *Oxford English Dictionary* this was a lotion used to treat gunshot wounds, an arquebus being a primitive gun. Ed]

There is a remarkable passage in *The Malefactors Register,* which is a collection of murder cases like this one:

> "From this time it seems that his Lordship applied himself to his favourite amusement, drinking, until he became exceedingly violent (for at the time of the commission of the murder he is reported to have been sober)."

Surgeon Kirkland arrived and Lord Ferrers told him that Johnson was more frightened than hurt. He described the steward as a villain who deserved to die, 'but now that I have spared his life, I desire you to do what you can for him'.

Kirkland examined Johnson and found the pistol ball still lodged in him. Ferrers expressed astonishment, saying that he had tested that pistol a few days before and it had driven a ball through a foot and a half of deal board.

It was bad news in those days to find a ball in the victim's body. Pistol balls were large and flew so relatively slowly that they dragged large fragments of clothing into the wound. This set up rapid infections which were often fatal when the wound itself was not.

We don't know if Johnson's wound was infected but Mr Kirkland was gravely concerned for the steward's life. In between bouts of boozing, Ferrers kept entering the sickroom, on one occasion to pull Johnson's wig, call him a villain and threaten to shoot him through the head. On another occasion he was only prevented by force from tearing off the bedclothes and striking Johnson. Mrs Clifford asked if Johnson could be removed to his own home, but Lord Ferrers said, 'He shall not be removed. I will keep him here to plague the villain'.

Towards midnight drink finally got the better of his Lordship who retired to bed, but not before telling Kirkland that he expected him to 'set the affair in such a light' as would prevent Ferrers being arrested.

Mr Kirkland felt that he owed a greater obligation to his patient. As soon as Earl Ferrers was asleep he had Johnson carried to his home on an armchair supported on two poles and guarded against any further attacks. It was in his home at Lount that Johnson died at 9.00 the next morning.

There followed a scene reminiscent of an old Frankenstein movie. As the peasants in those films rise up against Baron Frankenstein because of his creature's actions, now the villagers rose against Lord Ferrers, who had made a monster of himself. They advanced on Staunton Harold in an armed party to see the Earl making for the stables. A man named Springthorpe advanced on Ferrers with a pistol calling on him to surrender but thought better of his position when the Earl reached into a pocket. Thinking that Ferrers was drawing a weapon, Springthorpe failed to fire and allowed the murderer to escape into the house.

"A great concourse of people by this time had come to the spot and they cried out loudly that the Earl should come forth."

They continued to mill about the house and cry out for two hours, after which Lord Ferrers appeared at an upper window and asked what had become of Johnson. Told that the steward was dead, he declared it was a lie and ordered the crowd to disperse, then changed his mind and ordered that the house should be opened and the mob given refreshments.

He left the window saying that he would never be taken and the refreshments never materialised. The crowd remained and in about two hours a collier called Curtis saw his Lordship slipping away across the bowling green, armed with a dagger, a brace of pistols and a blunderbuss. Curtis seems to have been a hardier man than Springthorpe, for he walked up to the Earl and demanded his surrender. Curtis's resolution so impressed Ferrers that he gave up his weapons and surrendered, nevertheless remarking that he had killed the villain and gloried in it. He was taken to an inn at Ashby de la Zouch and when a Coroner's jury pronounced a verdict of wilful murder he was remanded to Leicester gaol.

Two weeks later he was removed to London so that he might exercise his right as a Peer to be tried before the House of Lords. He travelled in a six horse landau under armed guard and was lodged in the Round Tower of the Tower of London. Two armed guards remained in his cell at all times, another at the door, two at the foot of the stairs and one on the nearby drawbridge, all with fixed bayonets.

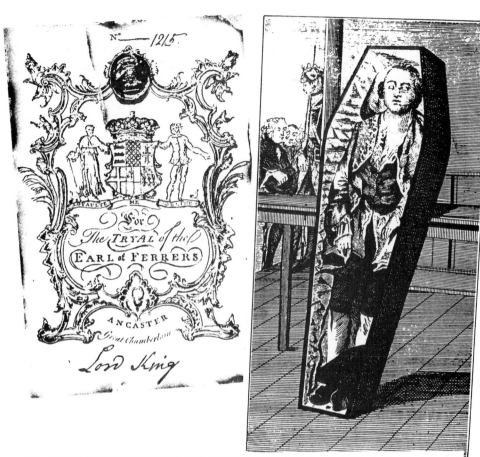

Contemporary sketches and something strange,
a programme or ticket for the 'tryal'.

They were not needed. The Earl was a model prisoner, 'his behaviour was decent and quiet, except that he would sometimes suddenly start, tear open his waistcoat and use other gestures which showed that his mind was disturbed'. This description sounds exactly like the 'horrors' felt by advanced alcoholics.

Mrs Clifford and daughters took lodgings in Tower Street. At first a servant shuttled to and fro with letters, until the authorities reduced the correspondence to once a day. Mrs Clifford was not permitted to visit Ferrers, though his daughters were. He also tried his hand at poetry:

> In doubt I live, in doubt I die,
> Yet undismay'd the vast abyss I'll try,
> And plunge into eternity
> Thru' rugged paths.

His trial before the House of Lords started on 16th April and took two days. Lord Henley, Keeper of the Great Seal, was created Lord High Steward to preside for the occasion.

Initially Ferrers called witnesses to show that he was not in his right mind, but none of them were able to put his insanity at such a level as to excuse the murder. Eventually his Lordship tired of the vain effort. He told the House that he was reduced to trying to prove himself a lunatic so that he might not be deemed a murderer. He confessed that his plea of insanity had been made only to gratify his friends, he had been opposed to it.

Without this late frankness the verdict would probably still have been guilty. He was sentenced to be hanged on 21st April and afterwards anatomised, that is, handed over to surgeons for experiments and teaching. In consideration of his rank, sentence was deferred until Monday 5th May.

On that last morning he dressed himself in a splendid white suit heavily embroidered with silver saying, 'This is the suit in which I was married and in which I will die'. He was permitted to take his own six horse landau to the scaffold at Tyburn. It was led by a body of Horse Grenadiers with carriages full of Sheriffs and Undersheriffs before and behind the landau. Behind came a mourning coach filled with the Earl's friends, a hearse to carry his remains to Surgeon's Hall and another guard of Horse Grenadiers.

A vast crowd gathered to see Laurence Shirley, Earl Ferrers, go to his death and they slowed the procession. At Holborn the Earl suggested that they might pause for a glass of wine and water, but the Sheriffs suggested that a stop might allow the crowd to 'incommode' him. So he went without a last drink and arrived at the gallows, mounting 'with composure and fortitude'.

He knelt with the Chaplain to recite the Lord's Prayer and asked forgiveness of his errors and pardon for his sins. He thanked the chaplain and Sheriffs for their services and gave his watch to Sheriff Vaillant, asking that he might be buried at Breden or Staunton Harold.

The performance was slightly spoiled when the Ferrers gave 5 guineas [£5.25] to a man he thought was the executioner but was actually the apprentice. The lucky one refused to relinquish the money when his master demanded it and a row broke out, which had to be silenced by the chaplain.

At last all was set. Ferrers stood beneath the cross beam with a white cap on his head, his arms bound by a black sash. The cap was pulled down over his face, the Sheriff gave the signal and the executioner caused a part of the platform to drop. An hour later his body was removed and taken to Surgeon's Hall whence it was released for burial three days later.

While awaiting execution Ferrers had made a will, leaving £1,300 to Johnson's widow, £1,000 to each of his illegitimate daughters and £60 pounds a year for life to Mrs Clifford. The will was invalid because it was made after conviction, but a similar arrangement was made.

'I should like to have my revenge.'
(Orgreave, Staffs 1895)

Frederick Bakewell of Orgreave was a grocer and farmer. Sixty six years old, he lived with his wife in Orgreave Cottage opposite Orgreave Farm. Part of the ground floor of the cottage formed his grocer's shop. It can have had little passing trade because it stood in a cul de sac giving access only to a field gate, though the main road was only about 40 yards away.

May 31st 1895 was a warm morning and at 9.00 the grocer and his wife sat at breakfast, the back door standing open. Mrs Bakewell was putting sugar lumps into a basin when her son, George Hackett, who was staying with the Bakewells, came down the stairs. He was a son of Mrs Bakewell's first marriage, 28 years old and an under guard with the Midland Railway.

George had just got up and, instead of joining his mother and step-father at the table, made for the open back door, probably heading for an outside toilet. He had scarcely reached the doorway when a shot sounded and the young man reeled back into the room, shot in the chest.

Screaming, he staggered across the room towards the front door, but as he reached it he was felled by a second shot and collapsed through the doorway.

Mrs Bakewell had no time to react to the attack on her son before a man stepped in through the back door and shot her husband twice in the back with a pistol, then shot Mrs Bakewell. Despite the warm morning, Mrs Bakewell wore a jersey, and the bullet passed through it and the underlying corsets to lodge in some wadding beneath, causing only a slight injury to her breast. As she ran to her son she believed that the intruder fired another shot at her.

Across the lane at Orgreave Farm half an hour before, Mrs Barton had been looking out of an upstairs window. She was watching her son in law, Mr Averill, as he set out along the road to Rugeley on his way to North Wales. As she waved to him she spotted a man among trees in the field behind Orgreave Cottage, apparently waiting for something. He seemed to be aware that Mrs Barton had seen him and moved out of sight.

By the time of the attack at the cottage Mrs Barton had gone downstairs, but was alerted by shots and screams. She looked out in time to see George stumble out of Orgreave Cottage and fall to the ground, then his mother run out to kneel beside him.

Mrs Barton and another neighbour, Mrs Lester, rushed to help, while the attacker made off through the Bakewell's back door. He raced across the corner of a field and over the fence of the Alrewas to Kings Bromley road.

Police officers arrived in Orgreave to find both Frederick Bakewell and his stepson dead of their wounds. Warnings were sent to Stafford, Burton on Trent and Lichfield and the surrounding area, and soon stories of a dark stranger began to emerge.

Mrs Bakewell thought she recognised the gunman. Several days earlier a tramp had called at the Cottage asking to buy some milk. He offered a shilling, but she refused it because he looked so wretched. She had been struck by his dark complexion and had enquired if he was 'a native', a term widely used then to mean exactly the opposite, a foreigner. He had said 'No' and gone.

From her description the Police were able to identify the killer as a convicted horse thief and burglar who had been released on licence but was wanted for failing to report to the Police. They circulated his particulars:

> **Thomas Bond**. Aged 30 years. Height 5' 8". Blue eyes, very dark hair and whiskers, which latter may now be partly shaven off. Very dark complexion. Dressed in dark cloth jacket, sacque shape vest of the same material and supposed dark brown corduroy trousers, old canvas boots with India rubber soles, round black hard felt hat, linen collar and black necktie."

Another branch of the Bakewell family might have had a brush with the killer. A dark stranger had peered into the window of a cottage at Kings Bromley Wharf, occupied by Mrs Bakewell's

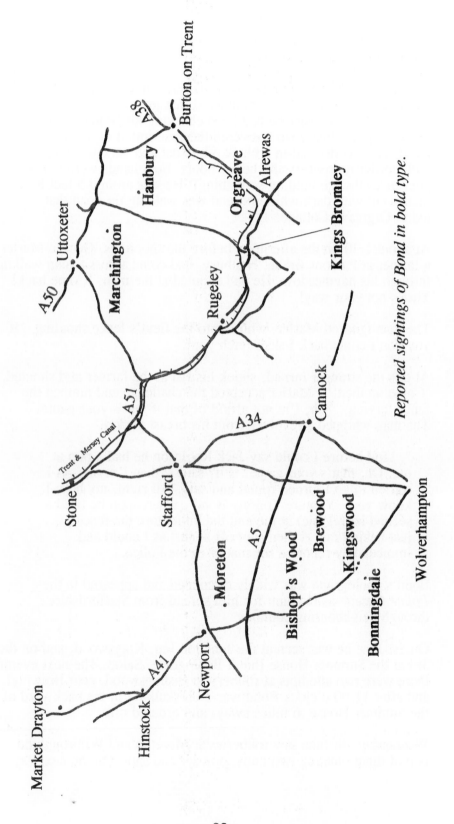

Reported sightings of Bond in bold type.

daughter and son in law. Their small son had called his mother and the man had gone away.

Thomas Pendry was a gamekeeper whose cottage was about a mile from the Bakewell's. He remembered that just before 8.00 on the morning of the murder he had been checking his brooding hens when he saw a man who answered the description of Thomas Bond. He was dressed in a black pilot coat and dark waistcoat with corduroy trousers and heavy boots. Both hands were in his pockets as though holding something. He was around 5 feet 8 inches tall with dark whiskers, and was walking the road that led to Orgreave Cottage.

At about 1.30 on the afternoon before the shootings, George Marler, a farmer at Parsons Brake, Hanbury, had come across a man walking through his haymeadow. He had shouted at the man, 'Come back! That's not your way!'

The man ignored Marler, who ran to the field's fence shouting, 'If you don't come back I shall fetch you!'

At this the stranger turned, shook his fist at the farmer and shouted, 'Come on then!'. Marler accepted the challenge and jumped the fence, crying, 'Oh, I'm not afraid of that if that's your game!' The man whipped a revolver from his breast pocket.

> "...and before I could say Jack Robinson he had a pop at me. Oh, that's your game, is it? said I, then I'm off. As I started to go I turned round and said, 'All right, my boy, I know you. You are Tommy Bond', whereupon he fired a second barrel (sic) at me and the bullet tore the fence just behind me. I then shot off as fast as I could and immediately reported the matter to the Police."

Bond's photograph was widely circulated and appeared in the *Police Gazette* as the hunt for him spread from Staffordshire through neighbouring counties.

On 1st June he was seen at the Junction Inn, Kingswood, and on the 3rd at the Summer House Inn at Boningdale, Salop. The next evening there were two attempts at robbery in Bishopswood, near Brewood, and after 11.00 o'clock Bond was seen skulking in the back yard of the Summer House, 6 miles away, and ordered off.

Wednesday 5th June saw robberies at Moreton and Wilbroughton one of them yielding two guns, powder and shot. On the next day a man was seen carrying a gun wrapped in oilcloth in the streets of Newport and local police thought it was Bond. On Thursday evening £10 was stolen from the home of Mr Cooper at Hinstock, one pound of it in 3 penny [.125p] pieces. Witnesses identified Bond's picture as that of a man seen hanging about the area earlier.

On Friday a man of Bond's description bought a ticket at Market Drayton station, paying the three shilling [15p] fare to Manchester in 3 penny pieces. Although the ticket was to London Road, Manchester, he left the train at Longsight.

Late on Saturday night two men were stopped at Baguley, some 6 miles from Longsight, by a man with a revolver who demanded money. One of them gave the robber 3 pence but his companion struck up the bandit's pistol with his stick. The robber fled and was later seen going towards Manchester.

Despite the apparent trail to Manchester, Staffordshire police kept their options open. They organised a search of Needwood Forest, knowing that Bond had lived rough there when evading a warrant for horse stealing. When a suspicious looking man was reported at Marchington, near Uttoxeter, they sent an Inspector and nine constables to search the area.

Public disquiet at the idea of a murderous tramp abroad deepened, bringing with it the inevitable wave of false sightings. Mrs Bakewell, however, seems to have been made of sterner stuff. She stayed in Orgreave Cottage with two relatives for company and is recorded as telling the police that she hoped Bond would not be caught. 'I have quite forgiven him for what he has done', she is supposed to have said.

It might have been this remark which started a local rumour that the shootings arose out of some kind of family dispute though there was not the least indication of this. It seemed clear that Bond, perhaps believing that Mrs Bakewell lived alone, had waited until Mr Averill was out of sight before moving in to rob the grocer's shop. He was startled into firing by the sudden appearance of George Hackett at the backdoor.

While the Staffordshire and Shropshire police sought him and Lancashire wondered whether he had travelled there, another force was keeping an eye out for Bond. His last conviction had been at Nottingham Assizes in July 1890 when he was sentenced to five years penal servitude for burglary and the theft of £1.3.6d [£1.17 1/2p] and a watch. Nottingham Police believed that they might see him again.

On the afternoon of 14th June a telegram to Staffordshire Police Headquarters confirmed that Nottingham had been right. Bond had risked walking past the Police Station at Hucknall Torkard and was spotted by the constable who had arrested him five years before. He was taken to Burton on Trent where an identification parade was organised.

For all her forgiving remarks, Mrs Bakewell trembled violently at the sight of Bond. 'That is the villain', she declared and turned away. As she left she turned back suddenly, as though to attack Bond, and had to be restrained. Nine other witnesses were able to identify Bond as the man seen lurking about Orgreave at the time of the killings, but none of the Shropshire or Lancashire witnesses picked him out.

Thomas Bond was charged and brought before Lichfield Magistrates in the Guildhall. A sizeable crowd assembled to watch his arrival and as he was brought in the women began to abuse him. He was quickly taken upstairs to the courtroom.

The Guildhall's upper room was and still is used for many other purposes so that it was not permanently furnished as a court. The two Magistrates sat behind a table and the dock was a portable affair that could be moved away when the room had less serious uses. Mrs Bakewell sat close to it, dressed in heavy mourning, and raised her veil to look at Bond. Suddenly she sprang at him, crying, 'That is the man! That's the villain! I should like to have my revenge on you, you wretch!'.

Restrained by friends, Mrs Bakewell had to listen to her deposition being read, then put up with cross examination by Bond, who had no lawyer. He seemed anxious to establish that she was wrong about the date of his first visit to Orgreave Cottage, but the widow kept repeating, 'You did it! You are the man. You know you were there!'

Bond was remanded in custody for a week and taken by train to Stafford Goal, blowing a kiss at a girl on the platform of Lichfield's Trent Valley Station. The following week he was committed from Lichfield Magistrates' Court to stand trial at the Assizes.

Details of his past began to emerge. He had been a criminal from an early age, first imprisoned at 15 for nine months for stealing 4s 10d [24p]. At 16 he served two months for housebreaking, at 19 fourteen days for begging and twelve months' hard labour for burglary. At 21 he entered the adult league, with five years for horse theft. Not long after he was convicted in Nottingham and received another five years.

He was released from that sentence on 8th May 1895, collected his prison earnings of 18 shillings [90p] at Stafford the next day and went to stay with an aunt and uncle at Hixon. He left them on 15th May saying he was going to Lichfield looking for work.

At Stafford Assizes several witnesses swore to his presence around Orgreave in the days before the double murder. Bond's counsel said this only established that the defendant was a tramp.

He poured scorn on George Marler's evidence of being shot at by Bond, suggesting that it would be strange for Bond to stay in the area where he had shot at someone. He pleaded with the Jury to be absolutely sure that Bond was not just an unlucky tramp, but this argument was destroyed by 12 year old Walter Heathcote.

On the fatal morning young Walter had been sent to fetch his family's milk. He had seen Bond twice, first at 8.35 as he went for the milk and again at 9.00 after he had collected it and delivered a letter. On the second occasion Walter had seen Bond approaching the open back door of Orgreave Cottage. He was quite certain of his identification. The Jury took ten minutes to find Bond guilty and he was hanged at Stafford Prison on 20th August 1895.

After his execution, a letter was released, one of those confect-ions regularly created by prison chaplains:

> "It is my desire that this should not be known to the public until after my death. I am lawfully accused and condemned of the crime of wilfully murdering George Hackett and his step-father. I beg of Mrs Bakewell and Mrs Hackett and those of whom I have injured by my crime to forgive me as I go to my death with a heart full of sorrow and ready to offer my life to God in atonement for these crimes. I also ask those whom I have injured by robbery to forgive me. especially my father, brothers and sister. I am fully convinced of the justice of my sentence and beg God to have mercy on my soul."

It seems doubtful that Mrs Baker forgave him again.

'A most terrible lesson.'
(Wolverhampton, Staffs 1908)

When it comes to scenes of violent passion involving a wealthy and prominent citizen and his lover, Wolverhampton may not be the first place that springs to mind. Even so, ninety years ago the sooty 'town of a thousand trades' became the stage for such a story.

The days between Christmas and New Year always seem the darkest of the winter, and if we no longer have many white Christmases, it is often bitterly cold. So it was on 29th December 1908, and Dr Galbraith of Wolverhampton must have been dreading a ring at his doorbell that would take him from the warmth and comfort of his home into a bleak night. When that ring came there was no question of not going out, the caller was a rich man, a brewer called Edward Lawrence.

Dr Galbraith went with Lawrence to his home, but refused to enter until another doctor had been called. This strange condition must have been laid down because of what Lawrence told the doctor on the way. Galbraith required an independent witness to what was found in the house.

In the dining room of Lawrence's home the two medical men found a young woman lying on the floor. Lawrence had already told Dr Galbraith that he had shot her. She had a slight wound in the right arm and a more serious one in the right temple, both of them from a pistol. She died soon after.

97

The police were called, but before they arrived Lawrence made comments which seemed to be an admission of guilt, then changed his attitude and said that the woman had shot herself.

The police arrived and noted that in the dining room a meal for two was almost untouched. They also noted that the revolver with which the woman had been killed contained four undischarged rounds and only one spent cartridge, as though it had been reloaded to give the impression that only one shot had been fired.

There was no doubt of the dead woman's identity. She was Ruth Hadley, a barmaid and Edward Lawrence's mistress. The brewer was a prominent man in Edwardian Wolverhampton and it was widely known that they were having an affair and that Lawrence had abandoned his wife and children. He was just as well known for drunken violence. His wife's divorce decree nisi had been granted on the grounds of adultery and of a brutal attack. He had even been fined for biting a policeman.

Lawrence was charged with Hadley's murder and appeared at Stafford Assizes in March of 1909. Witnesses told how the brewer had threatened his lover and shot at her on previous occasions. She had left him in September 1908, returning to him just before Christmas, and he had taken another mistress during Ruth's absence.

The maid who had served the couple on the night of the killing gave evidence of a quarrel when Lawrence accused Ruth Hadley of being drunk. She had denied it, making as though to fling the cruet at him. As the maid left the room she heard the key turn in the lock behind her. Her evidence seemed to look bad for Lawrence, apart from one small thing. She knew that it was Ruth Hadley who had locked the dining room door.

An old lawyer's maxim says that the defence's case is never in a better state than at the point where the prosecution evidence ends. However good the prosecutor's witnesses, they will have been damaged to some extent in cross examination and seeds of doubt may be sprouting in the minds of the Jury. Then the defendant must make his case, and that often becomes a downhill slide to a conviction.

Lawrence, however, had an advantage. He could well afford to brief the greatest criminal advocate of the period, Edward Marshall Hall. Readers of my other QuercuS book, *Midland*

Murders and Mysteries, will remember Marshall Hall's ing-
enious and successful defence of Ronald Light in the Green
Bicycle Case.

Marshall Hall called witnesses to show that it was not only Lawrence who was violent, Ruth Hadley had attacked and threatened
her lover on several occasions. What is more, when she returned
to his embraces that Christmas she was still deeply resentful
of his taking another lover during her absence.

For all his drunken violence, Edward Lawrence appeared well
educated and soft spoken when he gave evidence. He told how, when
he had accused Ruth Hadley of being drunk, she had flung crockery
and the fire irons at him. He had ordered her to leave his home
for ever and had gone to the bedroom to fetch the revolver which
he always kept under his pillow.

Returning to the dining room he had again ordered her to leave,
and had fired the pistol to frighten her. He was not aware that he
had injured her arm and had returned to the bedroom and hidden
the revolver under the mattress. Ruth had gone to the bedroom
and taken the gun before she turned the key in the dining room
door. She had, apparently, intended to kill him and, as they
struggled for the weapon, she had been shot.

Lawrence was not the first accused to tell a story of a lovers'
struggle over a gun ending in death. Others had not been believed,
but Marshall Hall showed how the brewer's account of events was
borne out by little pieces of evidence from other witnesses. There
was the disordered state in which the police had found the bed, and
the turning of the dining room key. Gradually Marshall Hall won
Mr Justice Jelf to his side, so that the summing up was largely in
Lawrence's favour.

An English Jury will usually do what they believe the Judge
wants them to do, and it took only twenty minutes for them to
acquit Edward Lawrence. Mr Justice Jelf told the brewer that
he had had 'a terrible lesson' and went on:

> "If you will turn over a new page in your life, you may yet
> have a happy time with your lawful wife and children, and
> then, perhaps, God will forgive you for the life you have
> led ..... I earnestly trust that what I have said will bear
> fruit in your heart and in your life."

Marshall Hall always thought his defence of Edward Lawrence was his greatest triumph, notwithstanding many other
headline successes. Whether it was worth his skill and trouble
and how much fruit the Judge's words bore is another question.
Three days after his acquittal Lawrence was charged with
assaulting a man in a Wolverhampton pub.

'Do you think I shall be hung?'
(Wychnor Bridges, Staffs 1816)

'What did we do before we had television?' people ask. The
answer is, a lot of different things. I doubt if people's view of
the world was much less accurate when it came without TV,
radio, magazines and newspapers than it is now. It was just
distorted in different ways.

Once there was a world where there were no televisions, no
internet, no cinemas, no radios, no magazines and precious few
newspapers, which two thirds of the population could not read.

Ann Statham lived in that world, in the village of Wychnor
Bridges, near Burton on Trent. It was a period when Britain
had just defeated Napoleon Buonaparte but was itself wracked
by social unrest. What Ann Statham knew about all that is
difficult to guess. She would not have known much about the
progress of the long war against the French, only what news
came to the village with travellers or was passed on by those
few who could afford and read newspapers. As she did not live
in an industrial town she would have heard little of the growing
unrest, though she might have learned of rising prices and
falling employment.

Where did a girl find her heroes in those days? There were no
pop stars, and though there were actors I doubt if Ann Statham
ever set foot in a theatre. Her choice was limited to the young
men of the village and an occasional stranger from the world
outside Wychnor Bridges.

In the spring of 1815, as Britain came to final conclusions with
Napoleon, Ann Statham found herself a hero. He was Thomas
Webster and he drove the mail coach on the Birmingham to Derby
stretch of the Birmingham - Sheffield route. Here was a man who
had seen more of life than the village boys, who had lived in big

cities and whose weathered face showed how he sat on the box of his coach for long days and nights, coaxing his team through wind and weather. She must have thought him a good catch, so much so that she left her mother's country cottage and moved to Birmingham with her lover.

By autumn she was pregnant by Webster and as the birth date approached she moved to Derby, where the child was born. The baby was about five weeks old when she decided to visit her mother, and Webster carried her on the mail coach from Derby to Burton. He left her there because she wished to see a Mr Mason, the constable.

Ann's mother's home was only about thirty yards from the coach road and Webster next saw Ann on the following day, 24th July 1816, as he passed through Wychnor Bridges. He did not stop on that occasion, but on Saturday 27th July he picked her up on his coach and took her to the Three Tuns at Barton Turnings. In the tavern he asked her how the baby was and she told him it was dead. He was surprised because the child had seemed well on the previous Tuesday. She said that it had died suddenly or in a fit, he could not afterwards recall which. The child was to be buried at Walton, she said, and Thomas offered to pay the funeral expenses, but she said she did not need money.

Webster called at the Three Tuns on the next day, and this time he saw the body of a young child in the storehouse. It had been taken from the canal. Thomas could not identify it with certainty.

Ann Statham had set out from Burton on Trent on Tuesday 23rd July, carrying the baby and heading for her mother's cottage. At Branstone she had met a butcher she knew, a William Challinor, but he thought she 'looked so ill' that he scarcely recognised her. She told him she had been lying in at Derby and showed him what he described as 'a nice fat, jolly, well looking child'. When she said that she was going to her mother's, but was very tired, Challinor suggested that she hitch a lift on a wagon that was passing at that time, but she refused.

She was seen next by Mary Palmer, who kept the toll house near Branstone where Ann stopped to rest. From the tollgate a short road led down to the canal, and Ann announced her intention of going that way. Mary suggested that she await a chaise which the tollkeeper knew was due to return from Burton to Lichfield. Ann said that a chaise driver would expect too much for a ride and she preferred to try for a canal boat whose boatman would charge very

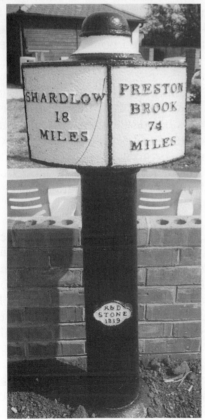

*Turnover Bridge and
a nearby milepost*

little or nothing. Mary, who you might have expected to know the local traffic, said that it was ten to one against Ann getting a boat, but she was adamant and went off to the canal.

John Deakin, a canal boatman, saw her standing at the canalside between Branstone Bridge and the Three Tuns. She was close to Turnover Bridge where the towpath changes sides and the horses had to cross the canal. He saw that she was wearing a dark dress and suckling a child at her left breast. There were two bundles lying beside her, one in a yellow silk handkerchief and one in a whitish wrapping.

Alongside Deakin's boat was one steered by George Thomas. Both of them went to the Three Tuns where they were staying the night, and about an hour later Ann arrived at the pub. It had now been raining heavily for about three quarters of an hour and she was drenched.

'You seem, mistress, to be sadly wet', said Thomas. 'Yes', she said, and he went on, 'I thought of asking you to ride, but I did not know which way you were going'. She said that it did not signify, that she had needed to call at a house by the roadside and had left the child there as she 'dared not bring it forward for fear it should be wet'.

Between 5.00 and 6.00 that evening a Mr Hodson of Barton was travelling the turnpike road (now the A38). Near Turnover Bridge he saw a woman in a dark dress beside the canal. It was raining heavily and she attracted his attention because she was walking slowly and stopping frequently. From a distance of about 50 yards he could not swear to her identity, but she had a dark dress and was carrying two bundles, one white and one of another colour. She did not have a child with her.

At 6.00 am on Sunday 28th July, Thomas Wootton, was steering a boat down the canal when he saw something floating about 100 yards below Turnover Bridge. He pulled the object from the water and found that it was a dead baby, dressed in a white bedgown and cap. He left it with Sarah Tompson, landlady of the Three Tuns. Charles Nicholls, Constable at Barton, was called and saw the body at about 7.30 am. He went immediately to Ann's mother's cottage.

There he found Ann having her breakfast, but she became agitated as soon as she saw the Constable. He asked her about her child and she said it was at Derby.

"I mean", he said, "the child which you were suckling on the towing path by the canalside on Tuesday last when the boats came past you and after that you came by those boats at the Three Tuns and on being asked what you had done with it you said that you had left it at a small house. That is the child I mean."

"My child is at Derby," she maintained.

"Ann you always told me your child was at Derby," said her mother, in whom a dreadful suspicion must have been dawning.

"I did leave it there, mother."

It was not enough for Constable Nicholls and he arrested her and took her to the Three Tuns. There Mrs Tompson said to her:

"Ann it is a pity that you did not come up by one of the boats that night "

"I wish I had," said Ann, "and brought my baby with me. I had a fit and it fell out of my hands into the canal. I waded after it as far as here," she continued, putting a hand to her knee, "but I could not reach it."

When she saw the bedraggled little body in the storeroom with mud clenched in its fists, she fell in a faint.

She was sent to Stafford Assizes, charged with murder, and Charles Nicholls junior escorted her there.

"Do you think I shall be hung?' she asked him. He said that he could not tell.

"I should think they cannot hang me" she said, "for no one saw me."

"I think you cannot tell," said Nicholls, "for there might be those eyes upon you that you could not discern."

"I am sure there was not," she replied, "for I looked round and there was no one by, nor anyone near."

At her trial the evidence was given of the sightings of her on the way from Burton. The defence did manage to elicit from Deakin and Thomas, the boatmen, that just past where they saw Ann the towpath had collapsed and fallen into the canal and that she would have had to pass this dangerous place, made slippery by the rainstorm, to reach the Three Tuns. Mrs Tompson of the Three Tuns said she had known Ann for years and never knew her to have a fit.

There was no evidence of how the child died, only suspicion created by Ann's contradictory stories. Mr Justice Park should have warned the Jury that her contradictions might arise from fear or a sense of guilt after the child's death, not a guilty knowledge of how the baby met its death. Instead he used them to persuade the Jury to convict, even attributing to her two stories told to Thomas Webster, when in fact it was Webster's poor recollection that gave rise to two explanations.

The judge referred to her remarks to Charles Nicholls junior as particularly damning, not seeing that they might be an account of an accident. He accused her of killing without motive, not even that of shame, for everyone who knew her knew that the child was Webster's and that he was willing to support her and their son.

It did not cross the judicial mind that lack of motive may be evidence of a disturbed mind. Postnatal depression was unheard of then. The Judge could only attribute her actions to a 'cruel, hardened and vicious disposition' when he sentenced her to hang.

Three other women were tried for the murder of illegitimate children at that Assize and were acquitted. Seventeen prisoners were sentenced to death, but only one sentence was confirmed, Ann Statham's. She acknowledged her guilt before her execution, but what that may have meant in her state we do not know. She had to be carried by two men to the gallows, where she died as the last prisoner to hang on the roof of the Lodge at Stafford Gaol.

Stafford's Shire Hall

'Respectable and indulgent parents.'
(Swindon, Wilts 1808)

Before the National Insurance Act of 1948 support of the poor within each parish was paid for by rates levied on the residents. The enthusiasm and generosity with which they discharged this obligation varied widely.

Two hundred years ago Rowley Regis believed that parishioners should be discouraged from becoming a charge on the parish, ending in the workhouse and a pauper's burial. To make the point, paupers were buried in a pit in the churchyard which was left open so that worshippers and passers by might see where improvidence led.

Young William Hawkeswood was bound for a memorable end of his own, but was unimpressed by the pit. In 1792 the youth was charged with 'secretly stealing sundry skulls and bones from an open charnel grave at Rowley Church'.

Hawkeswood's parents are described in contemporary accounts as 'respectable and indulgent', and his father's respectability saved the youth from a trial which could easily have sent him to prison. Instead a Stourbridge Justice of the Peace gave him a severe talking to in the belief that he could cure him of his strange habits.

It may have been his parents indulgence, rather than their respectability, that had bent the young man in certain directions. Hawkeswood senior was an undertaker at Pedmore, Stourbridge, and before his son was 10 years old he permitted him to help lay out the dead. Perhaps he thought this a proper beginning for a boy who would inherit the business. Little wonder that in later years William was described as having a 'morbid curiosity about the dead'.

His curiosity ran in other directions. His school record was good in several subjects, but notably in chemistry, so much so that, in his early 20s he became dispenser to Surgeon Fox senior at Kingswinford. He might have moved on into the medical profession but his lively mind let him down. He fell out with Fox by questioning the Surgeon's methods and was dismissed.

William returned to his father's business, embittered by his harsh brush with the world. He kept very much to himself, staying in his room and studying the ancient alchemists. These were the medieval magician/scientists who had sought the Philosophers' Stone, the secret of life itself.

The Pedmore Poisoner
a contemporary sketch

It was to advance his studies that he helped himself to spare parts from the charnel pit, for in his room he was building a human skeleton. He seems to have succeeded. After his brush with the law tales circulated about Hawkeswood having, 'from sundry remains assembled a complete skeleton and endowed it with the powers to shift itself in divers positions'. He had probably articulated his skeleton and perhaps added puppet strings to make it move. It was enough to set the darkest rumours flying and to damage his father's business.

It is not surprising that the simple folk of the area preferred not to take their dead loved ones to Hawkeswood, whose son played sinister games with bits of people. Instead the trade began to go to Andrew Reekie of Brierley Hill, patentee of a cast iron casket that was said to be proof against worms and 'resurrection men'. Burke and Hare were the most famous examples of men who dug up the dead and sold bodies to the dissecting rooms of hospitals. Indeed, with a known purloiner of body parts in the area, the secure casket must have been a considerable added attraction to those who wished to take their eternal rest undisturbed.

The dwindling custom and William's increasingly bizarre reputation made his parents decide on a fresh start else where. It was not very far, 6 miles away at Swindon, but they must have thought it far enough to leave the past behind. They bought a smallholding and Hawkeswood senior applied his coffin making skills to more general carpentry, purchasing a wheelwright and general carpenter's business.

William was forced to get work as a coachman with a Mr Parker, a job well below his abilities and ambitions. Parker owned a forge and farm lands and kept a large household at Chasepool Lodge, between Swindon and the Highgate. William Hawkeswood lived there in his own quarters over the coachhouse.

Apart from eating with the other servants, William spent his spare time in his quarters and resumed his study of ancient books and manuscripts. Mr Parker soon made a friend of his young coachman and took an interest in his studies, even allowing Hawkeswood to prescribe medicines for his chronically bad stomach.

All of this caused huge resentment and jealousy among Parker's other staff, the more so when a rumour passed among them that Hawkeswood would benefit considerably from Parker's will.

In March 1808 the authorities at Worcester were forced to respond to complaints from the Swindon area about the activities of resurrection men. A number of graves were opened in the area and eventually the Sheriff of Worcester sent his best Officer to see to the matter.

Sheriff's Officer Mark 'Grabber' Guier was an experienced thieftaker. It did not take him long to learn that young Hawkeswood had made free with parts of dead bodies in the past. He set out to trap him and his enquiries reached the ears of Mr Parker. It is said that a stormy interview took place between the two in Parker's study.

The following morning Elizabeth Cartwright, Parker's favourite servant, took her employer a cup of tea prepared for him by the coachman. Parker took a long drink from the cup and "perceived so unpleasant a taste that he declined to take any more and was soon afterwards taken ill. He immediately suspected that he was poisoned and gave directions that no expense be spared in detecting the villain, and that his body might be opened after death. About an hour later he was taken ill and died."

At a post mortem examination the surgeon detected white mercury in Mr Parker's stomach. He asked Hawkeswood to produce the cup and asked the coachman if he had tasted the tea. Hawkeswood said that he had, but he too had detected a bitter taste and had been violently sick. This, happened he said, in the presence of Benjamin Massey, the carter. The surgeon asked Hawkeswood to fetch Massey and the coachman left, apparently to do so. In fact he fled.

Now his father's indulgence reached astonishing proportions. He allowed his fugitive son to hide in his own house until a Coroner's Inquest named him as the murderer of Mr Parker, then he escorted him to Worcester and put him aboard the mail coach to Bristol.

By 1808 it was possible to travel in relative comfort by mail coach as an inside passenger, but William travelled outside perched on a seat on the roof. He was exposed to the weather and the worst lurching of the coach, so when the coach stopped at the Bush Tavern in Bristol he was perished. The landlord, Mr Townsend, saw him in the coachyard and told him to go inside and warm himself, but Hawkeswood disappeared.

Shortly afterwards a man entered the Bush flashing three shillings [15p] and telling how he had been asked by a stranger to show him to the Fleet Tender, the boat that took recruits to naval vessels. There the stranger had enlisted, receiving a guinea [£1.05] bounty, of which he had given his guide three shillings.

It was a small incident of no significance to a busy coaching inn, but it was remembered when Grabber Guier tracked Hawkeswood to Bristol and visited the Bush. Townsend took the Sheriff's Officer aboard the Tender and identified Hawkeswood.

William Hawkeswood stood trial for the murder of Mr Parker at Stafford on Monday 6th April 1808. It took only a short time to find him guilty and he was sentenced to hang at the scene of his crime.

Two days later the sentence was carried out, apparently on a tree in the vicinity of Chasepool Lodge. Hawkeswood's remains were passed to the surgeons for their experiments and, after they had done, the pieces were buried at the four points of 'Treosle' [probably Trysull] Crossroads.

If William Hawkeswood, a clever son of 'respectable and indulgent parents', failed to advance medical knowledge in life, he may have done something for it in death.

The beautiful graveyard of Rowley Regis parish church.

'He could thread a needle.'
(West Bromwich, Staffs 1933)

In the early hours of Sunday 27th August 1933, Charles William
Fox and his wife were sound asleep at their home in Moor Street,
West Bromwich. When a noise disturbed Mrs Fox she woke
convinced that she had heard breaking glass, and that there was
an intruder in the house.

Waking her husband, a 24 year old metal worker, she urged him to
go downstairs and investigate. Lighting a candle, he went down in
his vest and underpants while his wife watched from the landing.

She saw Fox look into the sitting room and then enter the room.
That was most probably because he had noticed that the window
was wide open.

As he went in the draught from the open window extinguished his
candle, and in the pitch dark he was attacked. On the stairs, Mrs
Fox heard a scuffle and a groan. Frightened, she called to her
husband, 'Charlie! Come back up, Charlie!' and retreated herself.
Her husband did not follow her immediately and she stood alone,
growing more frightened each second until Charlie stumbled into
the room. He reached out and flung his arms around her, then
without a word he fell dead. A knife was driven into his back.

Mrs Fox threw open the bedroom window and called for help.
Her screams alerted Harold Taylor, a printer coming off the
night shift, and in very short time two policemen arrived.
The intruder had gone but they could see that he had entered
by a window, removing one of the panes and leaving blood-
stained glass both inside and out. An examination of Charles
Fox showed that he had been stabbed seven times, one wound
puncturing a lung.

The murder of Charles Fox might very easily have passed
unsolved. Even if he had lived he could not have described
the attacker who ambushed him in that pitch dark room. His
wife never saw the intruder and no one was seen leaving the
house. Nor was there much reason why someone should burgle
the Foxes. Charlie had been a metalworker and in work, which
was rare enough in West Bromwich or anywhere else in 1933.
He supplemented his income by working as a door to door collector for the National Clothing Company, a credit company,

on Saturdays. The motive for the burglary that ended in murder seems to have been his previous day's collection of 14 shillings [70p]. That suggested the killer was local.

However, the Foxes were not the only targets of burglary that night. Not far from Moor Street a butcher called Newton slept over his shop in Bromford Lane, and he too had an intruder.

Mr Newton had found ample traces of his burglar. First there was the bowl of soapy water with Newton's cut throat razor floating in it, used and uncleaned, where the intruder had washed and shaved. Then there was a work basket taken out of a cupboard and a needle and thread used to repair something. Finally, having washed, shaved, mended his clothing and stolen a small sum of money, the burglar refreshed himself at the butcher's expense. He drank a pint of milk, and thereby sealed his fate.

There is almost nothing that takes fingerprints as well as glass. On Mr Newton's milk bottle the burglar and killer had left his signature, which Scotland Yard soon identified as that of a West Bromwich man called Stanley Eric Hobday.

Hobday was a small criminal in every sense, small in his crimes and small in stature. One witness described him as an overgrown dwarf. Having now killed, Hobday's only plan was to run. Stealing a car from near Bromford Lane he headed north. Scotland Yard approached the BBC and for the first time a police appeal for information was broadcast by radio.

The fugitive got as far as High Leigh in Cheshire when his driving let him down. The stolen Jowett Jupiter saloon skidded, rolled completely over and landed back on its wheels. Whether it was in running order after that manoeuvre we do not know. Perhaps Hobday became frightened of the possibilities of his own driving. For whatever reason he abandoned the car and struck out north-wards on foot, leaving an astonished farm labourer who had seen the accident, and a suitcase in the car.

He had made his way almost as far as Carlisle when he found himself sharing a country lane with a herd of cows. Hobday probably thought them no more than a nuisance, but he should have paid more attention to the cowman, Watty Bowman.

Watty Bowman owned a wireless set and had heard the Scotland Yard appeal broadcast. Looking at Hobday as his cows passed

him in the lane, Bowman decided that this might well be the
man the Yard were seeking. However, he had other things on
his mind, like getting the cows milked. It was a couple of
hours later that he told his employer about the stranger in
the lane, and the farmer picked up the phone to dial the
famous number - WHItehall 1212.

Once the Cumberland Constabulary knew that Hobday was
on their patch they soon found him and returned him to West
Bromwich, where the suitcase from the stolen car was waiting.

He was asked if he owned the case, and admitted it, saying that
he had been sleeping rough during the summer at Warstone Fields
but had been moved on by the landowner. He had left the case
hidden in some ferns at Haypits Woods.

Asked if he could describe the contents, he glibly listed some
clothing, a small tent, camping gear and a sheath knife. The
suitcase was unpacked in front of him, item by item. Everything
was there except the sheath knife. Was it the one that had been
driven into Charlie Fox's back? Was its sheath the one that had
been found between Moor Street and Bromford Lane after the
burglaries?

Hobday denied seeing his suitcase since he hid it at Haypits
Woods, saying that it must have been stolen from there. Its loss
he claimed, had been a considerable nuisance, making him sleep
in the open without a change of clothing.

Eventually a careful examination of the abandoned Jowett Jupiter
revealed Hobday's fingerprints on the starting handle. There was
no question now of saying that he had left the case in Haypits
Woods. He was charged and committed and stood his trial at
Stafford Assizes in November 1933.

By the time of the trial the police had neatly tied up the loose
ends. The sheath found between the scenes of the burglaries
fitted the knife with which Fox was killed, and a fellow camper
at Warstone Fields described Hobday as owning such a sheath
knife at that time. The shave and the mending at Newton's
home proved as fatal as the drink of milk, for the stubble on
the uncleaned razor proved to match Hobday's and the thread
left in the work basket matched a repair in his jacket.

Boldly his defending counsel, Sir Reginald Coventry KC, challenged the Crown evidence, not calling Hobday to give evidence, but insisting that the prosecutor had not made out his case. He told the jury:

> 'Think it over, gentlemen. Is it conceivable that any man, woman, or boy, after foully murdering another human being and with his hands still bearing the stain of blood, could calmly go off to Mr Newton's house and commit a burglary, sit down and shave himself, his nerves so calm that he could thread a needle and sit down and mend his clothes and then go off and steal a car?'

It must have been conceivable, for Hobday was convicted and hanged at Winson Green Prison in December.

'Trifle not with young mens' feelings.'
(Birmingham 1877)

Early newspapers were not the cheap, ubiquitous, bundles of pages that we use as chip wrappers, carpet underlays and window cleaning pads. They were small, often only four small pages, and they were expensive, partly because they carried a heavy stamp duty. As a result they only circulated among the middle and upper classes and tailored their news to this readership. The little pages were crammed with columns of small type reciting events in Parliament, foreign wars, ship movements, stock exchange prices and diplomatic manoeuvres.

More than two thirds of working class people could not read and had no access to newspapers and little interest in them. Occasionally radical movements would publish illegal and unstamped, newspapers for the workers, and some of them briefly reached large circulations, but sooner or later their publishers would be imprisoned and the journals disappear.

Those who wanted the entertainment provided by the modern tabloid papers, violence, mystery, sensational events and scandal, had to turn to the broadsides or broadsheets. These were single sheets of paper carrying one sensational news story, often a ballad or a set of verses on the topic and frequently an exaggerated woodcut. They were sold by 'patterers' on street corners, at fairs, race courses, and public hangings. Hangings were a particular source of both news and sales for the printers. The sheets cost a halfpenny or a penny [a quarter or half of 1p] and some of them logged astounding sales figures. The broadsheet recording the murder of Maria Marten in the Red Barn in 1828 is said to have sold more than a million copies, 'pretty tidy browns' (a lot of pennies) as a broadside seller would have said.

By the 1870s repeal of the duty on newspapers and the coming of high speed rotary printing presses cheapened and extended the newspaper trade. The working classes could now buy such cheap and dramatic publications as the *Illustrated Police News* and the *Illustrated Police Gazette*.

Broadsheets were dying out and had already become collectable curios. Charles Hindley published in 1872 a book of reproductions from his own large collection under the title *Curiosities of Street Literature*, reprinted by Broadsheet King in 1972. Many broadsheets survive. Collections can be found in the Birmingham Reference Library and in the Salt Library at Stafford, while many local museums keep a few.

Even so, in 1877 there were still some broadsheets which were knocked out by a few printers to record local sensations. In the spring of 1877 a sheet was selling on the streets of Birmingham, and its sad story was probably sung on street corners and in pubs:

> Draw near awhile you tender parents,
> List to what I will relate,
> It's of a tale of wicked murder,
> In Aston it was done of late.
> Poor Mary Saunders she was murdered
> By Frederick Baker now it's plain,
> Let's hope that of these cruel murders
> We may never read again.
>
> Now Frederick Baker is convicted,
> Dreadful, dreadful, is the doom,
> Doomed to die a shameful death
> In full health and manhood's bloom.

Frederick Baker was a 30 year old barman, a bachelor living in lodgings in Lichfield Road, Aston for which he paid 14 shillings [70p] a week. His landlady was Mary Saunders, a lady with two children who had been widowed nine months previously.

Single men in lodgings have long had a proverb that warns against falling for the landlady or her daughter. Such relationships often end with the lodger being evicted, and the view is taken that girl friends are easier to find than good lodgings. Frederick Baker ignored the traditional wisdom and set his cap at his 29 year old landlady.

> How Baker loved poor Mary Saunders,
> Sure no pen can it describe,
> But how she trifled with his feelings
> Drove this poor man nearly wild.

We do not know whether Mary responded to Baker's feelings, but we do know that there was a visitor to the lodging house to whom she showed friendliness. This was George Silvers who was the executor of the late Mr Saunders' will and followed the same trade as a glasscutter, and perhaps Mary went further than friendliness. It seems that she flirted with Silvers openly in front of Baker, despite knowing of Baker's feelings towards her.

Matters came to a head in January 1877. Mary and Silvers met one afternoon, apparently by chance, and went drinking whisky in the White Hart at Aston. Later they walked into the city and went to a theatre.

Baker came home to find his landlady absent and began to work himself into a rage of jealousy. Sure that his landlady was out with Silvers, he sent Sarah Stewart, Mary's servant, out to find Mary and bring her home, while threatening to kill Silvers if he saw him.

> Returning home that fateful evening,
> Nearly at the midnight hour,
> Accompanied by a man named Silvers
> That's why he murdered her, that's clear.

Silvers and Mary had gone from the theatre to another pub in Hill Street where they drank until past time for the 11.05 train, the last from the City to Aston. Eventually they came home by cab and Silvers took his leave of Mary outside her house.

Inside, the madly jealous Baker waited for her, and whatever drama she and Silvers had watched was nothing compared to the anger of the young barman. As soon as she entered he flew into a violent rage, abusing her while smashing ornaments and a lamp.

Even so, she was confident of her ability to calm the jealous lodger and dismissed her servant to bed.

The row ended, there were no further flying ornaments and Sarah Stewart must have believed that her mistress had worked her charms on Frederick Baker. Early next morning though, the servant found her mistress dead at the foot of the stairs, her throat slashed with a razor.

Baker was traced to New Street Station and arrested at Stafford, apparently en route for Liverpool and the wide open spaces of America. He freely admitted killing Mary Saunders and said that he had flung the razor away from a train at Aston Cross. 'It was Silvers brought me to this', he said with that traditional inability of criminals to believe that they have any responsibility for their own acts.

He was committed to Warwick Assizes where a plea of insanity was rejected. When the jury returned a verdict of guilty after only eight minutes, the judge told him he could expect no mercy. 'I don't expect any, my Lord', he replied.

Poor Frederick Baker stood his trial,
His counsel did the best he could
To save him from a wretched fate
For shedding Mary Saunders' blood,
But the jury found him guilty
And the Judge to him did say,
"For the crime you have committed
With your life you'll have to pay".

In a condemned cell he is now lying,
Thinking of his wretched end,
None to help him, none to save him,
Only God to be his friend.
May God above look down in mercy
On his sad and wretched fate,
And may he ask of God for mercy,
Ere, alas, it is too late.

Now all young people take a warning,
Think before it is too late,
If you're tempted to do a murder,
Remember his untimely fate,
And all young ladies take a warning
By Mary Saunders' sudden end,
Trifle not with young men's feelings
For to your destruction it may tend.

Doctor Johnson remarked that it 'concentrates a man's mind
wonderfully' when he knows he is going to be hanged. Certainly some of the most appalling ruffians seem to have found
some stability and poise before their execution. So it was with
Frederick Baker. Despite his ungovernable, murderous temper
and his fatal jealousy, a letter from the condemned cell to his
cousin at Tamworth suggests a different man:

"I am sorry to see you are so put about, but mind not - I am
going to a better land, and may meet my poor dear Mother
and Father and your dear Mother and your children there.
I am thankful to God that he gave me strength to bear my
trial so well, and to stand the sentence passed on me as
I did, but dear Cousin I knew well what it would be do
not think I have left everything to the last.

I have been preparing to meet this unhappy end for some
weeks now, and have every confidence to believe I shall
be fully prepared to meet my Saviour and those who have
gone before."

After more comments on his expectations of heavenly joy, he turned to his earthly situation.

"I am happy to inform you, dear Cousin, that I am pretty well under the circumstances, a warder is with me day and night and my food is very good, the chaplain comes to see me night and morning, so I'm not very lonely.

Taking all things together I am very comfortable but miss my tobacco, I have asked the doctor but it has not been ordered yet but I hope it may as it would be a great comfort to me while on earth.

Please write to Mr --------- and tell him I was pleased with my councillor (sic) he did well with the grounds he had to work on. I hope they are not getting up any petition as I would rather the law take its course.

In my box at Aston there is a paper that will tell how I have allotted my things and hope there will be no dissatisfaction among you, which just reminds me of what the soldiers did with our Saviour's clothes. You will find it in John, XIX, 23, 24 gladly would I welcome this unhappy death if as happy as the one those verses refer to but by God's help I hope to be washed in the blood that was shed for the redemption of all.

I will try to write a parting letter before I wish adieu, I will now close with wishing you a few lines (sic);

Farewell dearest cousin for now we must sever,
Ah, weep not, ah, mourn not for me.
May we all meet in Heaven, in glory for ever,
Oh, is there a triumph for me,
My Saviour that left the bright regions above,
The prisoners and captives to free,
With death's iron chains, how great was his love,
And yet there's a triumph for me.

From yours affectionately till death,

F.E.Baker."

One can only smile at the mention of the doctor authorising an issue of tobacco to a condemned man for reasons of health. You might also wonder at the efficacy of the prison chaplain in convincing Baker that, despite his sin, he was bound for glory, and Baker's vanity in plagiarising a revival hymn in his 'few lines' to his cousin.

Frederick Baker was hanged by executioner Marwood at Winson Green Prison on 17th April 1877.

Victoria Law Courts, Birmingham,
magnificent in pink terra cotta.

Midland
Murders & Mysteries

by Barrie Roberts

*,... she was surprised to find the inner door unlocked, the bar
door and windows unlocked ... and the pub's back door wide
open. ... Calling her employer's names she moved through the
building, wondering uneasily why there was no reply.*

◆

*There were two rows of cabbages under the farmhouse windows
and round the middle ones were traces of white powder.
Sergeant Smith wondered why a gardner would spread lime only
on the middle few and not on all the plants. Quickly they dug
into the cabbage patch and there found the ... naked and
doubled over body ... surrounded by lime ...*

◆

*,... his eye caught a gleam in the grass. Stooping, he found a
pair of gold rimmed spectacles. Nearby he found a set of lower
dentures and a woman's shoe. When he reached the churchyard
he saw that is showed signs of disturbance and, most
astonishing of all, the footstone of a grave was missing.*

◆

*Taking a torch the three went up the field, calling out for the
old man as they went. There was no response and the torch
revealed why not ... His arms were slashed ... his head was
battered and his own trouncing hook was still embedded ...*

244mm x 172mm, 116 pages
ISBN 1 898136 14 9
#7.95 from bookshops or QuercuS
(post free in UK)

WALKWAYS

Long Distance Routes
Step by step guides in both directions.

Heart of England Way (£6.95)
Warwickshire's Centenary Way (£6.95)
North Worcestershire Path & Midland Link (£5.75)
Birmingham to Aberystwyth Walk (2000)
Llangollen to Caernarfon Walk (2000)
Birmingham to Bala Walk (some time)

DaywalkS Footpath Networks
Networks of linked paths in rather special areas.

Cannock Chase (£4.95)
Vale of Llangollen (£4.95)
Wyre Forest (£4.95)

Strolls & Walks
A easy stroll and a longer walk from nice places.

Strolls & Walks from Picnic Places (Midlands) (£4.95)
Strolls & Walks from Cotswold Villages (£6.45)
Strolls & Walks from Midland Villages (£5.75)

Walks around…
Local walks for residents and visitors.

Twenty Walks around Rugby (£4.95)
Ten Walks around Coventry (£3.95)
Twenty Walks around Stourbridge (£4.75)

(No postal charge in UK)
67 Cliffe Way, Warwick CV43 5JG
Tel/Fax 01926 776363